Copyright Notice

I0464702

Dedication

You know how it is. You pick up a book, flip to the dedication and find that, once again, the author has dedicated a book to someone else and not you.

Not this time.

Because we haven't yet met/have only a glancing acquaintance/are just crazy about each other/haven't seen each other in much too long/are in some way related/will never meet, but will, I trust, despite that, always think fondly of each other...this one is for you. With you know what, and you probably know why.

(Apart from that, this is dedicated to Anne, Sam, Naomi and Tom, Sumera, Nabeeha, Omar, Ayaan, Tasneem and Inaayah with love and appreciation).

Steve and Nadeem

Contents

Welcome to Simple Sales for Superheroes!

We're delighted that you've made what we're sure will be the first of many heroic decisions, and that you've placed a little of your hard-earned trust in us, despite the very obvious fact that we've never actually met. We honestly believe that we can repay you by helping you along with our own hard-earned words of wisdom that are based on 50 combined years of experience at the sharp end.

The first thing that every superhero should remember is that every person out there has free choice and that every action has consequences (a useful nugget that will serve you well in the coming years). We completely understand that there are a multitude of books and sales training courses on the market, but you've taken a decisive action to take a look at what we have to say, and even if you ingest just a smattering of tips from each chapter, the consequent effects will absolutely help you to be heroically happy and successful in your sales career. And who knows, you may even save the world while you're at it.

This is not intended to be a definitive, scientific sales training guide. There are a plethora of systems and acronyms out there for a more formal type of training (which, due to copyright laws, shall remain firmly nameless). You should, as we have, continue to take the training wherever possible as the learning never ends. Sadly, there is no magic wand that will transform you into an instant superhero; you must pass many tests and rise above the occasional failure on your road to legendary status.

No, this guide is intended for you to dip in and out, taking note of whichever tips apply to you at defined stages in the sales, marketing and account management process. It is intended to be easily digestible, friendly and based upon the type of sales guide that *we* would want to read if we were donning underpants over our own tights.

In fact, we like to think that our book could have had several alternative titles;

- The Common Sense Book of Sales
- The Book of Easily Digestible Sales Tips
- What We've Learned and What Actually Works in Sales
- How to Make your Sales Stick (sticky sales, as opposed to a stick with which to beat your customer. Not a good idea. Ever).

You see, we believe wholeheartedly in Sticky Sales and Sticky Customers. While this may leave us open to certain unwanted and possibly lewd, potentially illegal, connotations, we will reward your early commitment to us by not insulting your intelligence in any way, shape or form.

Sticky Sales is our concept of sales that last. Sales that are repeatable. Sales that are earned by good practices. Sales that bond your customer to you. Because as sure as the sun will set again this evening, the best customer you will ever have is the one that you've already got. If you treat him with respect and professionalism and humour and responsiveness, he will bond to you like glue. And if you have *many* of these sticky customers who call *you* first whenever they need to fix a pain point in their organisation then, well...as the saying goes, you tabulate the arithmetic.

In the course of this book, we will impart and describe to you nuggets of information that we believe will help you through each stage of the sales process. This is not a scientific tome with role play and tests and scripted pitch. Everything here is based upon real experience. Experience that has taught us what works and what doesn't work. How to play the long game with consistent business rather than the short game and quick isolated wins. We have tried to avoid cliché where possible but have to humbly concede that any compendium of professional advice may sometimes veer this way.

So, who are we and who the hell do we think we are, having the nerve to even suggest that you might need a little help from us in your endeavours?

Well, I'm Steve Pinkney; my name derives from the French village of Picquigny in the Somme valley, near Caen. Ansculf de Picquigny arrived with William the Conqueror in 1066, and was awarded 80 manors across 11 counties as reward for his part in the conquest. His name is inscribed in the Battle Abbey Roll as a companion of the Conqueror and we

Pinkneys are descended from his bloodline.

 *And I'm Nadeem Mohammed, long time buddy and business partner of Steve; my name is common within the Middle East communities and means "a friend to wine and dine with", which is probably why we get on so well and connected in the first place.*

So apart from establishing that we are old mates, one of whom's ancestors may have inadvertently pinged Harold in the eye with a Norman arrow (allegedly) somewhere near Hastings a thousand years ago, you will be pleased to note that we also have extensive global sales and marketing experience in more recent times that will be more relevant to you.

We have worked together as colleagues, partners (and even as competitors) in and around technology sales, project management and service delivery since analogue times, when ISDN was short for It Still Does Nothing, mobile phones were the size of house bricks, and superheroes like you had to save the planet without the benefit of CGI.

We have each worked internationally for 25 years and successfully sold, delivered and managed multi-million-pound technology contracts, primarily to the global wholesale banking sector (although we have experience in many other markets). We have been Sales and/or Operations Directors for leading service providers with worldwide responsibilities, and have also run our own businesses.

Over the years, we have each recruited, trained and mentored sales professionals, project managers and engineers who have gone on to achieve enormous success. We have learnt from the great and the not so good. We have built our social and business networks upon honesty, respect and consistency. Sure, we've made mistakes along the way but that is actually a good thing. You will never learn unless you try!

When we initially discussed the possibility of writing this guide, we set ourselves a simple task. We wanted to impart common-sense tips for the sales superhero; the rookie just starting out in sales or the more experienced salesperson who may just want a quick refresher on what is important, without parting with £2,500 or so for a formal classroom-based course. Everything here is taken from our real-life experience and how we learnt, often the hard way, what works and what doesn't. You are free to disagree with our tips at any point, but even if you take just two or three elements from each chapter and apply them to your own style and personality, then we believe you will see a difference.

Your sales career is *all* about your customer. How many times have you heard that *People buy from People*? It is an absolute truth. We surround ourselves with people that we like. And why do people like us in return? Because the people that like us know that we put their interests first; we are interested in what they have to say, we care and we want to take their pain away. It's like falling in love over and over again. We're not suggesting that you declare undying love and devotion to your sales prospects - this would constitute a degree of weirdness and large security people removing you from their building – but a consistent empathy with everyone you meet will build you a fine network of friends, colleagues and customers. A network that you will enjoy and from which you shall reap rewards, both on a personal and professional level.

So, thank you for your interest in Simple Sales for Superheroes. We sincerely hope that you enjoy our guide as much as we enjoyed reminiscing and putting it together. Good luck, good selling, and may your heroic transition to bona fide Sales Superhero be everything that you hope it to be!

But before you continue, remember, with great power comes great responsibility.

(Steve, no. Just no – Nadeem)

So you want to be a Sales Superhero?

Is it a bird? Is it a plane? No, it's you.

(I give up – Nadeem)

The road to Sales Superherodom - *like that word!* - is laden with challenges that you must encounter and vanquish if you are to reach your goal. If your objective is to pay off the mortgage, take exotic holidays, drive the latest Mercedes, eat out when and where you fancy; or just simply to make money to safeguard your family's future, then sales is the road for you.

But like most things in life you will have to work for it. The rewards can be impressive but nothing ever comes easily; those naysayers who will call you lucky in the years to come? Forget it. Remember, you have to work hard to be lucky. You have to hone your powers to an extent whereby they become second nature; like driving a car. Or leaping a tall building.

Mistakes will be made. Signals will be missed. You will never stop learning. What you will do with practice, however, is gradually tilt the weight of probability in your favour. It will never be perfect; there are many other potential heroes out there, all of them trying to steal your thunder and take your commission. That's why you must be better than them.

Let's look at some of the Super Powers that you will need to translate into Sales Powers, but more importantly, how you will apply them in pursuit of prosperity.

SUPER POWER	SUPERHERO	SALES POWER	APPLICATION
Animal Morphing	Beast Boy	Adaptability	Adjust your persona to fit the situation in hand
Clairvoyance	Dream Girl	Empathy	Allow yourself to see the situation as others see it
Elasticity	Mr Fantastic	Effort	Stretch yourself; always do more than the competition
Fire Breathing	Ghost Rider	Assertiveness	Use controlled assertion in sensitive situations
Flying	Superman	Momentum	Move with purpose, agility and grace; keep your eyes on the prize
Ice Manipulation	Iceman	Calm	Maintain your cool at all times; the first to anger loses
Invisibility	Invisible Woman	Wisdom	Less is always more; know when to keep your counsel
Materialisation	Green Lantern	Preparation	Be mentally prepared and have all your tools to hand
Memory Manipulation	Professor X	Knowledge	Know your product, facts, figures and USP's
Object Animation	Giorno Giovanna	Eloquence	Concise eloquence brings your product to life
Physical Duplication	Naruto Uzumaki	Teamwork	Ensure your team is fully briefed and supportive
Self-Healing	Wolverine	Attitude	Look after yourself and keep everything in perspective
Super Endurance	Power Man	Longevity	Never give up, and look for long-term customers
Super Senses	Beast	Understanding	Learn to read people and their emotions
Super Speed	The Flash	Responsiveness	Respond quickly to every request and meeting
Super Strength	Incredible Hulk	Stamina	Long hours and late nights hurt; be kind to your body
Telepathy	Jean Gray	Listening	Listen closely to what your customer is really saying
Teleportation	Night crawler	Vision	Think ahead and trust your instincts; usually for the best
Time and Space Manipulation	Hiro Nakamura	Control	Don't rush the process; give people time to think
Wall Crawling	Spiderman	Composure	You WILL be driven up the wall at times. See Iceman
Web Spinning	Spiderman	Solutions	Provide solutions that will remove your customer's pain
X-Ray Vision	Superman	Observation	Observe people and their habits; you will adapt yourself

Developing a Superhero Mind-Set

The Sales Mind-set

SUPER POWER	SUPERHERO	SALES POWER	APPLICATION
Animal Morphing	Beast Boy	Adaptability	Adjust your persona to fit the situation in hand
Materialisation	Green Lantern	Preparation	Be mentally prepared and have all your tools to hand
Self-Healing	Wolverine	Attitude	Look after yourself and keep everything in perspective

- **The sale starts before you even leave home**

  Be positive about the day ahead and embrace the challenges. The Sales Superhero simply has to be in the right frame of mind to face the challenges of the day ahead. A positive frame of mind with the will to win will set the wheels of success in motion. The universe will work in your favour. Your body language will ooze confidence and people will believe in you and want to be part of who you are and what you represent.

- **Everyone has a story**

  Try to remember that every single person you will ever meet is fighting a battle that you know nothing about. Be kind and thoughtful whoever you are dealing with. People move about in the industry and you'll never know where you'll meet someone again. The last impression that you left will stay with them. If it's a good impression they are likely to call upon you again for your services.

- **Fix the pain**

  Your job as a salesperson is to find your customer's pain point, earn his or her trust, and solve it for them. Remembering those 3 points will stand you in good stead in the years to come. Treat every customer visit as though you're a consultant and not a salesperson. Your primary focus should be to understand their pain points first before you step in with your proposition.

- **Believe in yourself**

  Give yourself permission to win. Believe in yourself. You've been given this job for a reason – because someone else believes that you can do it. You sold yourself successfully to them; now go out and do it again. And again. Always believe in abundance. There is no lack in the world. It's all in your mind.

  Eric Butterworth put it very well in his book, Spiritual Economics: *"...you are a living magnet, constantly drawing to you the things, the people, and the circumstances which are in accord with your thoughts. In other words, you are where you are in experience, in relationships even in financial conditions, because of what you are."*

- **Pace yourself**

  A sales career is a marathon not a sprint. You will encounter disappointments along the way but you must keep going. Steady wins the race.

- **Just smile!**

  Smile and say *"Good Morning"* to 2 people on your way in to work; the ticket inspector, the coffee shop barista, for example. You'll be surprised how this simple interaction will lift your mood and prepare you for the day. And the recipient will be similarly enthused.

- **Learn from your mistakes**

  Never allow failure to enter your vocabulary. Redefine everything as a "learning experience" and focus on figuring out how to get different results. Never rest your chances on a single opportunity. Sales is a numbers game. If an opportunity doesn't materialise don't stress. Work on the remaining prospects until you hit the jackpot.

- **Treat everyone equally**

  Don't let emotion colour your dealings with people. Show everyone the respect that you would expect to receive yourself. We've been in situations where some of the humblest of people who some would perceive as "nobodies" turned out to be successful entrepreneurs with global enterprises.

- **Be cool**

  You will meet and work with many types of people; some awkward, some belligerent. Deal with it. Be calm and professional at all times.

- **Be humble**

  The salesperson who gets the order is the salesperson who got the last one. Even a small win will embed an innate confidence in you that the next customer will latch on to. But NEVER let it tip into arrogance – the Number One no-no in sales.

- **Use quiet confidence**

  In any meeting, develop and convey a subtle sense of *when will you buy*, rather than *will you buy*. This small alteration of attitude will help you establish a bond with your prospect.

- **Occasional defeat is inevitable**

  Don't be afraid to lose. It's the only way you'll learn. Winston Churchill once said *"Success is not final, failure is not fatal: it is the courage to continue that counts."*

  Every great figure in history, even modern day billionaires, have failed over and over again only to pick themselves up, learn where they went wrong, and move on to make their next attempt a success.

- **Look to the long-term**

  Be gracious in defeat and keep in touch with your prospect. This will always be appreciated and bring you new opportunities in the future.

- **Go easy on the humour**

  A sense of humour is important and will enhance your bond with customers and colleagues alike. But you're not a stand-up comedian. If you want to follow that path find an open mic night at a local comedy club. Remember, acting a clown in front of a customer will put you on the back foot. Customers will take advantage of you, particularly when it comes to price. Be professional at all times.

- **Don't knock the opposition**

  Negative selling is never a good thing. You will be tempted - my goodness you will be tempted! – but the golden rule is to never knock or criticise your opposition. Praise them as a viable alternative but focus on your product's known strengths against your competition's known weaknesses. Have a competitive analysis at hand to demonstrate that you've done your homework.

- **Be composed and conserve your energy**

  Above all, keep your composure at all times. The process of selling can be emotive and your superiors will often question your abilities in terms that you may find uncomfortable. This is because they themselves are under tremendous pressure. Keep calm and do not be drawn into an argument; they are a waste of your time and energy and no one wins.

- **Be aware of cultural differences**

  Always have understanding and ensure that you respect cultural and religious differences.

Clarity of Purpose

SUPER POWER	SUPERHERO	SALES POWER	APPLICATION
Super Senses	Beast	**Understanding**	Learn to read people and their emotions
Web Spinning	Spiderman	**Solutions**	Provide solutions that will remove your customer's pain
X-Ray Vision	Superman	**Observation**	Observe people and their habits; you will adapt yourself

- **Focus on your objective**

   "There is one quality that one must possess to win, and that is definiteness of purpose, the knowledge of what one wants, and a burning desire to possess it."

   Napoleon Hill

- **Be clear about where you're going**

   Clarity of purpose is vital for the achievement of success and for making dreams come true.

   Your dream or goal must be precise and clear, and should not be vague. While it's fun to daydream about being rich and successful, you have to know and define precisely what you want. Clarity of purpose is essential for every kind of success, for losing weight, getting a new car or travelling abroad. If you don't know what you want, how can you get it? When there is clarity of purpose, you know what steps to take, you focus on the goal, without wasting time or energy. Clarity of purpose is like focusing an intense source of light on your goal so that you see it clearly.

- **Set your goals**

  There's a saying *"if you don't know where you're going all roads will lead there"*. Clarity of purpose is an essential component of success. If you're not clear about what you want, how you're going to achieve it and by when, you're unlikely to make it at all. Make sure you have clear goals written out and review them every morning.

- **Create a 90 Day Action Plan**

  One of our mentors, Peter Thomson, said in a Mastermind Group that the best way to set goals is to portion them into 90-day chunks. 90 days is a period you can control. Beyond that it's almost impossible to know what will happen. The 90 Day action plan should clearly state your goal, the steps you need to get there, and how to write a determinant of your success.

- **Scoring a hat-trick is fine**

  Focus on no more than 3 primary goals in any 90 Day period. Any more than that and you're unlikely to achieve them. Focusing on just three major goals will propel you towards your primary goal in life.

- **Target the accounts that you want**

  Name the accounts that you wish to target. Another mentor, Jason Jackson, stated that you should create a TOP 100 Target List. These are the names of the 100 accounts that you want and need to target, and which you believe are the best fit for your product or services. For each account, find out the structure, the key decision makers, significant changes to that organisation, and understand the critical drivers in the industry that affect them. Then look through your contacts for someone that can get you an introduction to the company, as referrals are usually far better received than a cold call.

- **KISS Principle**

  The "keep it simple, stupid" principle is a term which indicates that the simplest solution or path should be taken in every situation. Keep your purpose, goals, proposition and pricing as simple as possible. You'll achieve huge success by following this, well...simple, principle in life.

- **Work while you sleep**

  Before you sleep, review your goals. Write down an action plan for the next day. Your subconscious mind will work through the night and give you clarity on the things you need to do. Your mind will even solve problems while you dream softly upon your fluffy white pillows. It's almost like having an invisible Personal Assistant in bed with you.

- **It comes from the top**

  Your Manager should be giving you a clear sense of what they want your company to stand for and accomplish, and communicate their vision to you regularly. Ensure that your goals and decisions are consistent with this vision. If, on the other hand, you do not or cannot agree with your Manager's style or objectives, you are working for the wrong company and should leave. Find a company where you will have a common purpose and mutual respect.

- **Balance your scorecard**

  One of the best tools we've used in our professional career is the Balanced Scorecard and a variant of this, the Personal Scorecard. The scorecard uses SMART metrics (Specific, Measurable, Achievable, Realistic and Timely) to measure progress, process and customer satisfaction. Apple Store and Google Play have many apps available, such as Andara and BSC Designer, so take a look, and use these to maintain consistency of purpose and adherence to your company ethos.

- **The outcome is everything**

  Focus wholeheartedly on *outcomes*, not *how* you will get there. For example, your desired outcome may be to target 30 Resellers in 5 Countries within 12 months and achieve revenues of £2m. You don't have to worry about the *how*. That will become apparent when you brainstorm the goal with your team. When you talk to prospects, they will want the reassurance that they are investing in a product that will grow and have longevity. They want to see you paint the big picture.

- **Get rid of distractions**

   Make a list of all the things that waste your time and simply put a stop to them. If you want to achieve greatness in life stop doing the things that drain you of your time. Everyone has 24 hours to play with. Unproductive people will waste all 24. Productive salespeople will master the art of focus and remove all time-consuming activities. These include Facebook, WhatsApp, YouTube and watching TV.

- **Remove clutter from your life**

   If you see anything around you that is there but doesn't serve a purpose get rid of it. Give it to charity or pass it on to a friend who may make better use of it. Decluttering your physical environment will clear your mind and allow you to focus on the important things in life. You'll enjoy working in simplified surroundings.

- **Remove the negative people**

  Surround yourself with people who will support your sales goals. Get rid of negativity. If anyone drags you down then get them out of your life. Surround yourself with successful, positive people whose company you enjoy. Spending time with negative people will breed negativity in you, and life is frankly too short to counsel people who like to gossip and moan. They'll be fine; let them gossip and moan to someone else. Eventually they'll find someone who shares their dark cloud, and they will be happy together.

- **Maintain a journal**

  Write in it every single day without fail. You only need 5 minutes max. Write what you want to achieve for the day. Make a note of what you're grateful for. List what you'll do better the following day. As you reflect on your journal in the future, you'll be able to look back and figure out how and what brought you the success that you desired.

Perception is Reality

"Looking good, man!"

SUPER POWER	SUPERHERO	SALES POWER	APPLICATION
Super Senses	Beast	**Understanding**	Learn to read people and their emotions
Invisibility	Invisible Woman	**Wisdom**	Less is always more; know when to keep your counsel
Clairvoyance	Dream Girl	**Empathy**	Allow yourself to see the situation as others see it

- **Your perception is *your* perception**

  Often used in marketing and leadership guides, the phrase *Perception is Reality* can be seen as a trite soundbite that means many things to many people. But that is actually the point.

  What you perceive *is* your reality. Your environment and the way that you approach every situation is based on *your* experiences, *your* background, *your* hopes and fears. This will ultimately have a direct and constant effect on the way you work and the way that people relate to you.

- **Reputation is everything**

  In sales, your reputation is everything. Think about how you would like to be perceived and be consistent, whether you are dealing with friends, colleagues, customers or competitors. Ultimately, you are looking for respect from others. From respect comes trust.

- **Everyone's perception is different**

  Never forget that people see what they want to see. Their personal perception of life will be different to yours. Your job is to quickly find the level at which you meet, and then bond through mutual understanding of what must be done to remove any barriers. This will be achieved by eliminating the pain point or area requiring a solution, i.e., your product or services, and making *your customer's* perception become reality.

- **Have belief and be content**

  If you believe in yourself, others will believe in you. If you are content with your life and actually like yourself, others will be relaxed in your company.

- **Be clear and concise**

  Everything is open to interpretation. This is a fact of life as we are all projecting our own personal perception values to the world, which in turn is our reality. Be clear and concise to cut through people's fears over how they are being perceived.

- **People want to be liked**

  What someone thinks of you is important but they are actually more exercised by what you think of them. Everyone, deep down, just wants to be liked.

- **Adapt to people and situations**

  In sales, you must subtly change your perception to fit all scenarios. But you are not an actor or an impressionist. You are who you are and you should not disturb people's opinion of you too much or trust is lost.

- **Trust your instincts**

A vital skill to learn is not hearing what *is* being said, but what isn't. Reading between the lines sometimes gives you an idea of what is really going on. But don't over-analyse everything.

- **Everyone is different**

  Try not to compare yourself with others. No two lives are the same. No one can feel what you feel. Comparing yourself with others can breed envy and that is another complete waste of your time and energy.

- **Albert Einstein and Henry Ford**

  We were discussing the importance of perception one day and, and in an effort to prove our point to each other, resorted to our interpretations of famous quotations by Einstein and Ford. We say interpretations because that, in truth, proves the point. We all have our own individual thought patterns so it doesn't matter if our interpretations differ from the original. What is important is that you try to understand your customer's perception value and focus on this to fix his pain point. As the great men (genuinely) said;

  "Reality is merely an illusion, albeit a very persistent one." (Einstein)

  "Either you think you can or you think you can't and either way you're right." (Ford)

Marketing for Superheroes

Your Value Proposition

"Yep! I save people. That's what I do!"

SUPER POWER	SUPERHERO	SALES POWER	APPLICATION
Object Animation	Giorno Giovanna	**Eloquence**	Concise eloquence brings your product to life
Time and Space Manipulation	Hiro Nakamura	**Control**	Don't rush the process; give people time to think
Web Spinning	Spiderman	**Solutions**	Provide solutions that will remove your customer's pain

- **Be clear and concise**

  A value proposition is a promise of value to be delivered. It's the primary reason that your   prospect should buy from you. Your value proposition is a (usually non-verbal) headline or tagline that must be easily understood and convey simple benefits to your customer and target market. It explains how your product solves a problem or improves their situation. Quantify your benefits where possible. Explain how your product is different.

- **Use Visuals**

  Include a strong visual to explain what you offer. An infographic is normally a good way to describe your offering visually. Within the graphic clearly show the areas your product touches, the benefits, industry facts, and anything else that will give the reader an instant understanding of your value proposition.

- **Clarity trumps persuasion**

  A lack of clarity creates friction, friction creates confusion, confusion leads to back button clicks. Be absolutely clear in everything that you say.

- **Use language your customer will understand**

  A strong value proposition uses the language that your customers use, and clearly explains what the product can do for them. Consider this example found in Peep Laja's excellent article on value propositions:

"Revenue-focused marketing automation & sales effectiveness solutions that unleash collaboration throughout the revenue cycle".

From reading this, do you know exactly what this product is and what it can do for you? Not likely. Or does this work better?

"Create beautiful emails in minutes"

- **Is this for me?**

  The questions most people have in their mind when they first visit a web site are;

  "Am I in the right place? Am I going to find something useful for me here?"

  People want to understand if it's for them, how they'll benefit, and why they should use this service instead of one your competitors.

- **Don't be too clever**

  Many sites jump too fast to efforts of persuasion by leading with their differentiators or testimonials. They're important pieces of the puzzle but not as a leader. Or worse, they try to be clever or funny, but really don't say anything at all.

- **Get to the point**

  The purpose of a good headline is to get customers to read the second line. The best taglines get your attention and raise curiosity or surprise. But we're not *all* copywriting experts. If in doubt, always go for simple clarity. Clarity leads to higher conversions.

- **Look at how others do it**

  ProductHunt is a daily leader board of the best new products and presents the reader with a list of great taglines. You're browsing the homepage, skimming over the list and trying to decide which one is interesting enough to click through. Be self-observant, think about which products you click on, and why? ProductHunt's short descriptions in a competitive environment are a great place to quickly see what separates a good value proposition from the bad.

- **Try it yourself**

  Reverse engineer this with your own value proposition. If a user was to see your product amongst the ProductHunt list, what tagline would best describe what you do and make prospects more inclined to click through?

- **Know your market**

  Crafting a great value proposition requires a deep understanding of what is unique about your company and your products and services. It's all relevant to your target market. You need to understand;

    a.   their demographics
    b.   the language they speak
    c.   how to talk to them
    d.   why they buy

- **Theodore said it**

  In the 1960s, Theodore Levitt, esteemed professor at Harvard Business School, said, *"People don't want a quarter-inch drill, they want a quarter-inch hole."* He was talking about describing benefits, not features.

- **A simple formula**

  Dane Maxwell's "Copywriting Checklist" outlines a formula for an *'Instant Clarity Headline'*.

  Formula

  End Result that Customer Wants **+** Specific Period of Time **+** Address the Objections

  Example

  Recruit 2 Top Producing Agents Each Week without Cold Calling or Rejection

- **Don't be difficult or dumb**

  Steer clear of vague superlatives, hype and jargon. Words like "easy, okay, sick or smart". Do you think your competition goes around saying they are "hard, difficult, worse or dumb"?

- **Bite size chunks**

  Break your proposition into chunks that make it easier to understand and easier for you to sell. If you lump everything into one meandering mess of a proposition it will be become unclear what you actually do.

  A number of software products describe themselves as offering an ERP solution, but what does this actually mean for the end customer? If these companies were to break the proposition down into smaller chunks, and clearly describe the value proposition they are offering in simple terms, they would be far more likely to attract higher quality leads.

- **Talk to your clients**

  Everyone understands the importance of knowing what your customers want, and listening to them, but if you want real clarity you should ask them directly. Ask your clients for feedback. They are only human and will be more than pleased to talk about themselves and their pain points.

- **It's been emotional**

  Emotions influence every human beings' decision making process, so get some emotion into your offer. People respond to emotion, not logic, when they're buying.

- **The 6 Emotional States of Buying**

  All buying decisions are based upon a variation of the following six emotions;

1.	Greed	"If I do this now, I will be rewarded."
2.	Fear	"If I don't do this now, I'm toast."
3.	Altruism	"If I do this now, I will help others."
4.	Envy	"If I don't do this now, my rival/competitor will win."
5.	Pride	"If I do this now, I will look smart."
6.	Shame	"If I don't do this now, I will look stupid."

  As a sales superhero, you must understand your customer and how your value proposition can be adjusted to suit his emotional state at any given point. This is crucial at every point of the sale, and does not just relate to your value proposition. The importance of emotion is key to all that you do in sales.

- **Get some outside help**

  Creating a powerful value proposition can be difficult to do by yourself. Get a view from the outside. Use your connections to speak to marketing people whom you respect, and who have effective copywriting skills.

Effective Marketing Strategies

SUPER POWER	SUPERHERO	SALES POWER	APPLICATION
Flying	Superman	**Momentum**	Move with purpose, agility and grace; keep your eyes on the prize
Super Endurance	Power Man	**Longevity**	Never give up, and look for long-term customers
Teleportation	Night crawler	**Vision**	Think ahead and trust your instincts, usually for the best

- **To social media or not to social media**

  Marketing has changed dramatically over the years since the advent of social media. We're now bombarded with adverts on almost every social media platform that Google touches. The point is, with all the options available, you must choose only those that are appropriate for *your* business.

- **Snail Mail**

  Believe it or not, the good old post has a far higher opening rate than anything else. While everyone else is battling to be seen and heard on social media, the successful marketers are combining their strategies with Postman Pat. People are, quite frankly, bored and/or suspicious of so many SPAM emails and links to click. So our tip for you is to think about a free article, book or information product that you can send to your prospects.

- **Get it out there**

  There is a piece of advice that our dear friend and social media expert Jacqueline Briggs once gave us. She said that the reason so many business owners fail to market their products effectively is because *"they're simply too worried about how the market may perceive them. They're afraid that they may say something ludicrous and be laughed at."*

  In fact, the opposite is true. The important thing is to get your message out there. Don't waste time. Your message may not resonate with everyone who reads it but isn't it better to get your message out than to leave it sitting on your computer?

- **People want to be included**

  Creating a constistent buzz in the market is important for three reasons;

  1. It creates curiosity in potential customers and investors
  2. People want to be part of something exciting and successful
  3. It builds confidence in the minds of potential customers

  Make a list of everything new that's happening in your business. Write a press release and publish it on PR platforms (many are free). Write about new features of your product. New hires, new offices or new resellers that have joined your business. But just do it. That's the key.

- **Video works**

  Educate customers about your product or service using videos. Videos are more likely to be viewed than text so use them effectively on your website to show customers how your solution can solve a problem. And don't worry about giving too much information away. The more you give, the more you'll receive. Leave your competitors to play catch-up in the background.

  To create videos use tools like GoAnimate, Camtasia Studio or Livescribe. There are loads on the market that make the process easy. If you're not comfortable creating videos or doing voice-overs yourself (have a go, we love doing it) then use resources on Fiver.com or UpWork to get someone else to do it for you. These platforms offer affordable resources across a wide range of areas for your business.

- **Who are you targeting?**

  Identify your target market. Create a profile of your ideal customer - or as Peter Thomson (Peter Thomson International) calls it - a Customer Avatar. What type of person buys this service most frequently today? Why do they need your service? What is their job function? If it's a consumer product, where do they live? How old are they? How much do they earn? What other factors make them a likely customer? Where are they most likely to look for the service or hear about it? Who might they ask for a referral?

Once you answer those questions, ask yourself another; "*Where should I be networking or what should I be doing to make myself known to that potential customer or to people who give the prospect referrals?*" After you've answered the questions, act on them.

- **Promote what people actually want to buy**

  Promote what your customer wants to buy. Customers don't want the service you perform. They want the solution to a problem or benefit your service provides. Think about it. A plumber's customers are not interested in plumbing. They want a leaky pipe fixed. A web developers' customers do not want a database or design. They want a website that will make them look good, get found in search engines, and help them attract new customers. If you need help in figuring out what your customers are actually buying, just ask them. Write down their answers and get better results from your marketing by focusing on the particular problems that your service solves or the benefits it provides.

- **Be a trusted resource**

  Make yourself a trusted resource to prospects and clients. People like to buy from people they know and trust. They don't like anything "sold" to them. Provide information that will help them make the right choice. If you write articles make them educational, not blatant sales pieces. Make your material available via multiple sources such as web, PDF download or video. If you have the resources available to you, you should also consider podcasts and webcasts.

- **Strategic partnerships**

  A strategic partnership is an alliance between two organisations, usually based upon one or more common business contracts, which does not necessarily require a legally binding partnership. Clearly, the best companies with whom to strategically partner are those that provide complementary services to your own, and which will serve a mutual purpose in winning the business.

  The best partners are also those that you like on a personal level, and with whom you enjoy working. We've tried the alternative. It doesn't work.

- **Social networking**

  Create accounts on LinkedIn, Facebook and Twitter. Update your status on a regular basis, connect with everyone you know and reach out to new people through the people in your network. Leverage existing relationships to create new ones and to get your foot in the door where you'd like to do business. The key here is to be consistent with your output. Try and get an article published every two weeks. If you don't have time to write an article yourself, outsource it to a suitable freelancer on Upwork.

- **Doing interviews**

  Do you have any friends or acquaintances in the media? A worthwhile tactic is to pitch some ideas about how you can teach people what you know, whilst simultaneously helping them to connect with their audience in a more effective way.

- **Public Speaking**

  Look for gigs where you can tell your story of how you got where you are today, or you could educate on a specific topic that's of interest to people. It's very important to note that you absolutely *cannot* sell from the podium. It will destroy your credibility very quickly.

- **Picking up the Phone**

  It sounds like such an easy answer, but most people would rather have their teeth pulled without anaesthesia than cold call people. We believe that consultative or referral sales are the best approach, but if you absolutely have to cold call, then the trick is to have confidence and a purpose before you pick up the phone, and be able to NOT take it personally if they don't want to talk to you. Remember, cold calling is a numbers game and it can take 99 "no's" before you get a single "yes".

- **Don't sell. Educate**

  The key with most of these tips is not direct promotion; rather, it is education and getting people to see your expertise by sharing in your knowledge, your time, and your energy.

- **Time and money**

  Marketing of all kinds requires an investment to create momentum, whether it is time or money. Marketing with money doesn't always take much time, but marketing effectively without money almost always requires a significant amount of time. Take these pieces of wisdom with the understanding that these WILL work with proper dedication and focus, and you'll start to see them pay off in no time.

- **Free is the way to go**

  Have you ever thought why it is that artists are happy to publish their songs for free on YouTube? The paradox is that they sell more records by giving free access to their material than they would by using traditional marketing methods. So you should consider what you can give away for free to build trust, knowledge and confidence your products and services.

Marketing Collateral

SUPER POWER	SUPERHERO	SALES POWER	APPLICATION
Invisibility	Invisible Woman	**Wisdom**	Less is always more; people's attention spans are short
Object Animation	Giorno Giovanna	**Eloquence**	Concise eloquence brings your product to life
Teleportation	Nightcrawler	**Vision**	Think ahead and know what your tactical objectives are

- **Embrace the marketing thing**

  As a sales superhero fighting the daily battle for orders, you might consider the need for good marketing collateral a necessary evil. But we believe that you should fully embrace this area and work with your marketing team to ensure that your message is consistent and powerful across all media. Marketing is not just about having a decent brochure to leave on your customer's desk (that he'll probably never read). It's about making sure that he gets a consistent message and information flow from you as he considers your products and services.

- **You can do it**

  We have launched successful businesses from scratch and with little or no budget. Through trial and error we have become pretty damn proficient in creating eye-catching marketing collateral that contains that all-important facet, *Impact and Momentum*. And guess what? As a creative sales superhero blessed with your undoubted powers of observation and decent English language skills, you will come to enjoy the process much as we did, and still do.

- **Tactical is good**

  Whilst this section stresses the importance of working with your in-house marketing experts, it is often the case that you will have no such person in your organisation, or they are engaged upon more *strategic*, corporate work that maintains your company image or market position.

  However, you should always consider more *tactical* sets of collateral that you may produce yourself to support short, targeted campaigns whilst conforming to your company's standard profiles i.e. logo, typeface, colour scheme and so on.

- **Plan Your Marketing Campaign**

  The first step is to clearly map out your marketing tactics. This doesn't have to be a complex exercise. A simple plan highlighting expectations and clear steps to get you to your goal is all that is needed. In fact you can map a marketing campaign on a single sheet of A4.

  Know your audience and keep the content relevant. Think about the best possible means to get to your customer and keep the process simple. There's no need to jump onto every social media platform if you're trying to sell tractors to farmers.

- **Tell a story**

  Tell a story so that people understand who you are, what it is that you do, and why you're doing what you're doing. It helps you build your brand following. Effective marketing collateral can be the difference between a near-sale and a loyal client for life.

- **Create a professional corporate style**

  Get the help of an expert designer to create an image that represents who you are. There are a number of good freelancers you can get from UpWork (formerly Elance). Or better still, ask around for a recommendation of a designer that one of your contacts may have used.

  Make sure that all your collateral stands out with a consistent, professional and highly polished feel. We've worked with leading design agencies, including bha (brightleyhodges.com), who advised us on the importance of creativity, style and presentation to achieve maximum impact.

- **Revise your material**

  Lay all your collateral out and read it thoroughly. Revise content that no longer applies and add new content that is relevant and hits a chord with your prospect. Read the latest material on the industry that you are trying to target and ensure that you have facts and figures that add a bit of spice to your message. Find out what the leading analyst firms like Gartner, Forrester, and IDC are saying about your target industry and about the future of your market.

- **Make the message simple**

  Every piece of marketing collateral should clearly communicate a particular message to your clients. By extension, you also have to structure your message in a way that makes sense to your prospects. People are scanners, so it is vital to be able to hook them into your content with a well-organised, effective design. This means high-impact graphics, killer headlines, bulleted copy and short paragraphs. Simplify the design, skip the jargon and define clear and unique selling points.

- **Go through the customer journey**

  How do you get your customers to go where you want them to go on your website, or when they receive collateral from you? It's all about what motivates your customers; what are their needs, their hesitations, their concerns? Being able to align with your customers in terms of what you want them to achieve when they visit your website is essential. Imagine you're the customer and follow the process step by step until you're comfortable with it. Then analyse the results to ensure you're getting the desired results.

- **Use quality material**

  Over the years, we've come across presentation material, brochures, and business cards that spell image disaster. They look cheap and simply tell a prospect that you're not interested in business but are there to....well, get by. On the flipside, companies that make an effort and invest in their brand, flick the quality perception switch instantly in the minds of a customer. We were once presented with a business card made of metal. Now that's something you don't forget very easily.

- **Make marketing material visually appealing**

  They say you shouldn't judge a book by its cover, but let's be honest ... a pretty cover doesn't hurt when it comes to your marketing. That's why whether you're creating lead generation content, social media content, calls-to-action or infographics, your marketing material should always be as visually appealing as possible. The problem is, creating all these beautiful visuals is not everyone's speciality. Design software can cost an arm and a leg (plus all the classes you need to take to learn how to work the damn stuff).

  But there's good news, there are plenty of free and easy-to-use tools out there that can make you look like a master designer. Check out the App Store and resources that are available on the web. You'll find tons of clever software to make your material look good, although our preferred approach is to just let a designer get on with it.

- **Integrate physical with digital media**

  Given the ubiquitous use of smart phones and tablets, you should give your customers the choice of reading or viewing your material on both print and electronic media. Use video where you can to emphasise your message. Offer a PDF download, video option or text on a website. Some companies offer links to webinars which were previously hosted. Another great idea is to offer your customers a combination of media. Just try to mix it up a little. Surprise people.

- **Make sharing easy**

  Social media plays a large role in content marketing as one of the key distribution vehicles for content. In addition to advertising and email marketing, social media shares of content via sites like Facebook, LinkedIn, Twitter, Pinterest, Google+, Tumblr and other platforms allows good content to spread: the modern equivalent of word-of-mouth marketing. This is why you must ensure that you have links to as many social channels as possible on all your online material.

- **Print is Not Dead**

  We're flooded with emails every single day. Unless you have a cracking title an email is unlikely to be opened. Many companies are now resorting to snail mail. If you think about it, you're more likely to open a letter sent to you than an email.

Educating the Customer

SUPER POWER	SUPERHERO	SALES POWER	APPLICATION
Elasticity	Mr Fantastic	Effort	Stretch yourself; always do more than the competition
Memory Manipulation	Professor X	Knowledge	Know your product, facts, figures and USP's
Web Spinning	Spiderman	Solutions	Provide solutions that will remove your customer's pain

- **Education, Education, Education**

  Did you know that educating customers is one of the most effective marketing methods but it's not yet become an essential part of the sales process? You have to remember that your customer is bombarded with information on a daily basis. If they are to fully appreciate what you are proposing to them then you'll need to put some effort into *teaching* them the benefits of using your solution over anything else on the market.

- **The Silent Giant Killer**

  What a brand doesn't say is just as important as what it does say. The business graveyard is littered with companies that failed because they forgot that their prospects had to believe they needed the product before they'd ever buy it. They simply forgot to educate their customers.

- **Make education a key component of your marketing plan**

  Although it may sound strange, educating your customer should be a pivotal piece of your sales and marketing plan. Educating the client is one of the best ways to increase your sales and turn people into long-term customers.

When someone is first thinking about buying a product or service, they probably don't know very much about it. That's going to make a prospect hesitant to buy the product. Remember, lack of clarity turns customers away. If the prospect is not 100% certain they're getting a good deal, or whether the product they're considering is good enough, or what their other choices might be, they will be uncomfortable, and this gets in the way of the sale.

- **Work on the customer's emotion**
  If, on the other hand, someone takes the time to help you learn more about the subject, it not only gives you the confidence you need to make a purchase, but also earns your trust and loyalty.

You'll be more likely to go back to that source of information again.

What kinds of things can you educate your client on?

Think about the Apple Store. The fact is their advertising is so powerful that before you walk into one of their shops you've already made your choice. But that aside, when you walk into an Apple Store, there are experts to show you how every product works. They have workshops to guide you through everyday activities that you can manage on one of their devices for free.

These workshops then help to drive someone to part with their money.

What can you do to help your customers do the same?

- **Write a thought leadership piece**
Knowing about your product and company is a great place to start, but customers also want to know more about the field in general. They want to know about their other choices, and whether it's a field they should be looking into in the first place. A great option here is to come up with e-books or reports in which you discuss the market sector in which your products and business operate.

Use a recognised name like Gartner to back up your supposition. This will add clout and will nurture an element of trust in what you're writing about.

- **Customer education videos**
On the web, customers and prospects are often looking for knowledge, not necessarily a product to buy at that particular time.

To build a deeper relationship with their customers, FedEx uses video to teach best practices when it comes to shipping. Deffinity.com uses videos to teach users the benefits of using their project management software. Sticky Sales Ltd are releasing short training videos on Udemy and their website.

Video is clearly becoming a leading method in educating customers. They can access videos in their own time, not when *you* want them to. Plus they can watch videos on their mobile devices whilst on the move.

- **Build an online community**
  Educating resellers, certified users and decision makers has always been embedded in the Cisco business model. Building a community of educated followers has helped Cisco grow its brand beyond just networking technology. Targeting IT savvy learners, the Cisco Learning Network features wikis, games, simulations and other resources.

  While participating in immersive learning experiences, users interact with Cisco staff and other users and start to view the technology world as a Cisco world.

  Think about how you can create such a community for your product or service. But make sure you have the manpower to deal with the queries, suggestions and other points made within that online community.

- **Use Webinars**

  In recent times, webinars have become a popular means to communicate with customers. This is a powerful medium to reach out to existing customers and channel partners spread across the globe. They are also used to share information about products or services and their various applications.

  The webinars also serve as excellent media for industry thought-leaders to share their experiences, and news of the latest industry trends and standards. Customers find these web sessions useful and informative and are willing to participate in them, as there is no compulsion to purchase any products.

  Even if you don't get the level of attendees you expected, the webinar can be used off-line and added to marketing collateral on your website (you don't have to mention how many people actually attended the webinar). There are excellent books available online that will teach you how you can engineer and make your webinars successful.

- **Provide free training**

  This is similar in principle to the Apple Store workshop idea. Providing free seminars on relevant business issues can help to build trust in your product and emphasise your experience in overcoming such problems.

- **Share relevant experiences. Use stories**

  Sharing experiences through storytelling can help customers make decisions and solve problems. Your customers will be drawn into a story if they understand up front that the story is essential to a problem they are facing. Relating the story character(s), points or principles to your customers' situation will keep them tuned in. Cutting out aspects of the story that have no relevance to them or impact on the outcome is a policy to which you should always adhere.

- **Keep it simple and to the point**

  When educating your customers, keep the conversation relevant to their current or future needs and cover what is important to them. Education is not showcasing your knowledge on everything but the kitchen sink, it is about skilfully communicating information that impacts or has the potential to impact your customer given their circumstances.

- **E-Newsletter**

  Sometimes, you might have product updates and innovations that you wish to share with your customers. E-Newsletters are excellent for maintaining contact with your customers and keeping them posted about your new product offerings, industry updates, and information pertaining to your specific domain, events, product launches, webinars or any of your product innovations.

Customers genuinely appreciate any information that adds value to their knowledge and business.

- **Have you created value?**

  It is important that you create value in every sales call or meeting. Today's consultative approach to selling means that your customer should be getting value from you every single time that you meet, even though he may not yet have spent anything with you.

  We've found it useful to ask ourselves, post-meeting, whether our prospect or customer would have been happy to pay for our meeting and our time. If so, how much value would he place on the education he has just received? Kind of focuses your mind, doesn't it?

Lead Generation Strategies

SUPER POWER	SUPERHERO	SALES POWER	APPLICATION
Flying	Superman	Momentum	Move with purpose, agility and grace; keep your eyes on the prize
Super Senses	Beast	Understanding	Know what people want, and when they want it
Teleportation	Nightcrawler	Vision	Think ahead and trust your instincts; know what works

- **Jumping through hoops**

  We once attended a sales seminar which talked about getting your prospects to jump through hoops. The first hoop would be large and easy to jump through, nothing complicated and easy to tackle. The next hoop would be smaller and more difficult to jump through and so on.

  The hoops represent the commitment that a prospect needs to make before they buy your product or service. Generally the first hoop is free. The next may also be free or exchanged for a small fee (referred to as a trip-wire). And so the process goes on until you convince your prospect that what you offer is valuable enough for them to part with a large amount of their hard earned cash.

- **The magic formula**

Generally speaking, there is no one magic formula to generate a ton of leads. If there were, we'd all be millionaires and there would be a lot of bright young marketing graduates looking to retrain. Granted, for some businesses there are more effective ways than others, but on the whole, long-term *effective* lead generation comes down to a combination of the following seven criteria:

1. Define Customer Profile
2. Define Target Lists
3. Make Contact
4. Present and Qualify
5. Establish Referral System
6. Manage PR and Blog Campaign
7. Create Buying System

You need to employ all seven approaches in order to generate the right kind of know, like and trust building that will attract your ideal customers. Indeed, 80% of your time should be spent in using and perfecting this "magic formula."

- **The 3 C's**

In order to better understand why this blended approach makes sense let us introduce the 3 C's of lead generation:

1. Cost

2. Credibility

3. Control

Each one of the lead generation trio offers you some advantage in one or more of the 3 Cs. By using them all, you get the perfect mix. Let's look at these elements in 3 examples.

a) Advertising

Potential high cost, often lower credibility, high (in fact, ultimate) control. You can turn the ad on and off when you choose. In fact, control is the best part about advertising; you can launch a targeted promotion on the day you want or need more leads, and then turn it back down again when you don't.

b) Public Relations

Cost can be low, credibility is high; often a tiny mention can bring more leads than a full page ad in the same publication. Readers tend to love the third party endorsement. Control can be low as you can't really dictate when and if you will get any publication space.

c) Referrals

Again, cost can be very low. Credibility can be low dependent on the source of referral but is more often high. Control is also out of your hands and based on your ability to educate sources properly.

Each constituent part of the lead generation trio has pros and cons, but employed as a unit they have the power to help you create the kind of marketing momentum that builds long term success.

- **Inbound Lead Generation**

  From a tactical perspective, a marketer needs four crucial elements to make inbound lead generation happen:

  1. **Offer**

     An offer is a piece of content that is perceived high in value. Offers include e-books, whitepapers, free consultations, coupons and product demonstrations.

  2. **Landing Page**

     A landing page, unlike normal website pages, is a specialised page that contains information about one particular offer, and a form to download that offer.

3. **Call to Action**

   A call-to-action (CTA) is either text, an image or a button that links directly to a landing page so people can find and download your offer.

4. **Form**

   You can't capture leads without forms. Forms will collect contact information from a visitor in exchange for an offer.

- **Use element of scarcity**

  If you look at the principle of supply and demand, you'll notice that when supply is limited, demand goes up. Scarcity has a psychological influence on us, making us want something even more if there isn't enough to go around. Scarcity is great because it creates a fear of shortage, and thus a sense of urgency.

- **Limited Time Offers**

  Limited time offers are among the most popular in the scarcity category. Just think about your average car dealership. Practically every commercial is a limited time deal.

  "Get 0% financing before it's gone!"

- **Limited Quantity Offers**

  When something is of limited quantity, it suddenly becomes more unique or exclusive. In some studies, limited quantity or supply offers have outperformed limited-time offers. Why? Because it's hard to tell when an offer of limited quantity will suddenly become unavailable, while a time-based offer has a known end time. Limited quantity offers are great for not only getting people to say "yes" to your offer, but to avoid procrastination completely.

- **Limited Time and Limited Quantity**

  Groupon is the perfect example of the use of both tactics. All Groupon deals end within a certain time frame, and they limit the number of people who can buy a Groupon. That's a powerful combination. The site also packages these scarcity tactics with discounting, which is another great value-add, especially for e-commerce businesses.

- **Focus on creating a brilliant title**

  Brian Halligan, CEO and co-founder of HubSpot, once said that *"you can have a great offer with a bad title and no one will download it. But if you have an amazing title, suddenly everyone wants it."* Yes, people do judge a book by its cover. If your offer is a piece of content, such as a whitepaper, e-book, or presentation, put your effort into creating an amazing title.

- **It's the Buy-Cycle not the Sales-Cycle that matters to your prospects**

  The internet has changed the way that technology buyers make purchasing decisions. These buyers are now much more proactive when seeking out solutions to business issues, relying less on the vendors' salespeople to provide the information upon which they base their decisions.

  TechTarget and Google suggest that 95% of technology buyers conduct their own research online, starting with search terms about solving particular business issues. This takes the form of 3 phases;

  1) **Awareness Phase**

     Of the buy-cycle; when they are discovering 'How to solve XYZ'.

  2) **Consideration Phase**

     Where specific solutions and/or vendors are researched.

  3) **Decision Phase**

     Where online behaviour is characterised more by 'Brand' and 'Comparison' research. It's worth noting that around 70% of these browsers will go on to buy a related product or solution within the next year.

- **Buyers dictate how the sale progresses**

  As buyers learn more about the solutions that can solve their business issue, they start to narrow down their research and create a shortlist of potential vendors. It is at this stage that buyers indicate a willingness to engage with a vendor's sales team i.e. after they have researched solutions and/or have an understanding of the competitive vendor landscape and offerings.

  Buyers these days are unreceptive to cold calls or uninvited sales pitches. But if vendors manage to "get on the radar" of prospective buyers during the "awareness" and "consideration" stages of the buy-cycle they stand a much better chance of being able to help shape the criteria for a purchase as well as influence budgets.

- **Plan a Webinar**

  Webinars are a great way to quickly generate new leads. All you need to host a webinar is a tool like GoToWebinar (free for 30 days), an idea for a presentation that your target buyer personas would enjoy and a few hours to prepare.

  Almost any company can run webinars which their prospects would find useful, and once you've created your concept it's just a matter of sending an email out to your contact database and promoting your webinar as best you can throughout your website.

- **Create a LinkedIn PPC (Pay per Click) campaign**

  Most sales people and marketers will have at least some experience using LinkedIn to market their product and organisation. It may be through participating in groups, building their own personal networks, or something similar.

  Few have had much success with LinkedIn PPC campaigns. However, if your company has at least one whitepaper or e-Guide that is useful to your prospects, you can quickly setup a LinkedIn PPC campaign of your own.

  Your PPC campaign can be highly targeted - whether that means targeting people at specific companies, or UK men aged 18-35 with web development skills currently at 50-100 employee companies.

- **Setup a new landing page**

  What's a landing page? It's a page that contains a form designed with one single purpose: to convert a visitor into a lead. Landing pages can help you to convert more visitors to your website into known leads, which you then have an opportunity to convert into sales.

  The more landing pages you have, the more opportunity you have to convert your visitors.

So take a step back and have a think about the landing pages you've put together. Are there new ones you can create which are targeted towards specific personas, segments or new problems? Could you create a new offer which would convert a demographic which visits your website that is currently underserved?

- **Optimise Call to Actions (CTA's)**

  A CTA (call-to-action) is any button, image, or text on your website which inspires your visitors to take an action. Every page of your website should contain at least one CTA, because every page of your website should have a purpose: an opportunity to convert.

  Take a look through your website and see if there are any pages that could be improved by adding an additional CTA, or by revising an existing one. Could you test new copy in your CTA's to see if they perform better? Could you add a secondary CTA to some of your pages to convert visitors who aren't yet ready to take up your other offer?

- **Improve Your Customer Avatar**

  Over time, your customer avatar becomes outdated. Your target market is always moving: they're consuming content in new places, facing new challenges and encountering fresh problems. Not to mention, your company is moving too. Is the persona you were most focused on a year ago still the best one to target now?

Are there additional personas you need to think about? Your marketing needs to adapt.

Developing customer avatars isn't a one off "*set it and forget it*" exercise. The most effective marketers will be constantly reviewing their buyer personas to ensure that the marketing material they're creating is still on point. It's amazing the impact that a regular review of your avatars can have on the efficacy of your overall marketing strategy.

- **Breakfast seminar**

  Holding regular complimentary breakfast seminars aimed at updating and building awareness of your products and services is an excellent, and inexpensive, way to generate leads.

  Whether it's a breakfast seminar or a lunch briefing, offering your prospects a relaxed environment where they can sit back, have a coffee and a croissant and listen to your proposition is generally a good way to start building rapport with a prospect.

  To get prospects to the breakfast seminar you will require a good lead generator, which could be a free downloadable report or something similar.

- **Small batch TARGETED direct mail**

  We know we all want to do that mega blast thing and have it rain leads, but in reality that just doesn't work, unless you're selling a low-value, high-usage commoditised product. The more personal you can get, the better.

You will receive far greater results targeting 50 or 100 ideal prospects a month and reaching out with a personalised letter outlining one highly actionable idea than any other form of mass communication out there.

- **Interview and Podcast**
  If you want to work with CEOs of mid-sized manufacturing companies then create a show where you interview successful CEOs of mid-sized manufacturing companies, who just happen to be happy to share their journey to success with your listeners.

  Okay, maybe you don't have any listeners (yet), but your guests don't need to know that and while you are building your following you'll be getting some valuable content that helps you build authority, and just might land you in a conversation with a prime prospect.

Managing the Sales Process

The Seven Steps of the Sales Process

SUPER POWER	SUPERHERO	SALES POWER	APPLICATION
Elasticity	Mr Fantastic	**Effort**	Stretch yourself; prepare, create impact and momentum
Memory Manipulation	Professor X	**Knowledge**	Know your product, facts, figures and USP's
Web Spinning	Spiderman	**Solutions**	Provide solutions that will remove your customer's pain

Plan and Prepare

- Review your product knowledge
- Create and memorise your Elevator Pitch
- Research and understand your prospect
- Create an action agenda

Open

- Initial meeting
- Propose your action agenda
- Control and assess

Gather

- Find your prospect's pain point
- Gather information
- Qualify the opportunity

Present and Prove

- Deliver a compelling response

- Present your proof that pain will be fixed

- Offer a POC (Proof of Concept)

Adjust

- Adjust the solution if required

- Handle objections

- Trial close

Close

- Ask for the order

Follow Up

- Thank and confirm

- Upsell and Cross-sell

- Manage account opportunities

Develop your Product Knowledge

SUPER POWER	SUPERHERO	SALES POWER	APPLICATION
Materialisation	Green Lantern	Preparation	Be mentally prepared and have all your tools to hand
Memory Manipulation	Professor X	Knowledge	Know your product, facts, figures and USP's
Web Spinning	Spiderman	Solutions	Provide solutions that will remove your customer's pain

- **You need credibility**

  Your customers need to feel comfortable that you know how to help them. They are investing in you as a person. Respect that and learn about your products and services.

- **Know your competition**

  Be aware of your competitors and how they sell their solutions. The person you are selling to will make it his job to know your competitors. This is critical for him to maintain his own credibility within his organisation, and to achieve his KPI's (Key Performance Indicators), targets and bonus.

- **Never, ever bullshit**

  No-one like to say that they don't know. Your customer knows that you're a salesman, a facilitator. He understands that you are not a technical architect or an engineering guru. You are the point person, there to bring in expertise as required. He will respect you more if you admit that you don't know something; but ensure that you tell him who does have the answer, and when they can provide it.

- **Transfer features into benefits**

  Don't be tempted to fall back on the salesman's last refuge, the dreaded Feature List. At some point the customer will certainly need to know (or at least have a basic understanding of) the weight, dimensions, memory and capability of your solution, but he can read that in the brochure. What he's looking for is your advice on how the solution will fix his pain point. How does a particular feature relate to his precise problem?

- **"Which means that..."**

  Keep this phrase in mind whenever you are pitching your product or service. Assuming you have successfully discovered the pain point that needs to be resolved, name three (always an easily digestible number) relevant features and how they would help him.

For example, your prospect has told you that his biggest concern is managing his customers; spreadsheets are cumbersome and full-scale Enterprise CRM's (Customer Relationship Management systems) are expensive and complicated.

Think about your solution and apply benefits to features;

FEATURE		BENEFIT
Compatible with Safari IOS, Android, Google Chrome, Windows and Explorer.	"which means that"	Sticky CRM will work on any device or tablet that your sales people prefer.
Simple CRM functionality with tile buttons on home screen.	"which means that"	Your salesman can update his records as soon as he leaves his meeting, with his thumb".
Built-in templates synced with Outlook Calendar and Email to confirm/thank/reschedule meeting and propose next steps.	"which means that"	Your customer will receive an immediate response and your records will be updated in real-time, so the sales cycle is accelerated.

- **Knowledge breeds enthusiasm**

  The more you develop your product knowledge, the more enthusiastic you will become. If your customer sees that you have genuine belief in your product, he will be more likely to buy from you.

- **Handle objections**

  You will be more equipped to handle and answer objections if you are confident in your product knowledge. If your customer is looking for a certain element, or has a specific pain point to be fixed and you are not aware of it in your product, just make sure that you shut the door quietly on the way out.

- **Use your product**

  It goes without saying that the best way to learn your product is to use it yourself. And don't stop there. Instead of watching cute cats on YouTube in the evening, take a trawl through your competitors' offerings. Download a trial if it's available. This is your career we're talking about. If you don't learn it someone else will, and guess where the commission will go?

- **Get to the USP**

  You are selling in a competitive market. The harsh truth is that the majority of your competitors' products and services will do pretty much what your own product and services do. All of the goods and services in your sector are there to fill an essential need, to perform a required function. However, there will be Unique

Selling Points where your solution will be vastly superior. Product knowledge is all well and good but you must know your USP's and use them.

- **Ask questions and apply your knowledge**

  While it is understood that you will be inordinately proud of the depth of your product knowledge, a customer meeting is not an opportunity to list every feature and benefit that exist on the planet. Ask your client where his pain points are (see section on Qualification Process) and apply the relevant benefits that relate directly to him. If you *are* tempted to list everything you have then your client will know that you haven't been listening to him, and trust is lost.

Create and Memorise an Elevator Pitch

"Now that's what I call an elevator pitch!"

SUPER POWER	SUPERHERO	SALES POWER	APPLICATION
Flying	Superman	**Momentum**	Move with purpose, agility and grace; keep your eyes on the prize
Materialisation	Green Lantern	**Preparation**	Be mentally prepared and have all your tools to hand
Super Speed	The Flash	**Responsiveness**	Respond quickly to every request and meeting

- **So, what do *you* do?**

  When you are meeting new people in your business or social life (and the plan really is to meet as many as you can) at some point in the conversation when they feel comfortable with you (a very good start), they will pose the inevitable but welcome question;

  "So, what do *you* do?"

  As an eager salesman looking for leads and prospects or even a new friend, you have struck gold. This is your chance to make a quick impact and open up a potential sales opportunity. You have 20 seconds to make a new friend.

- **It's a free lead**

  We can't emphasise how important it is that you get this right. Just think how much time, money, effort, energy and planning is involved in your company's marketing programme. How many mailers, offers, introductions and calls do you have to make to uncover just one decent lead?

- **Don't sell.....yet**

  Your elevator pitch should rattle off your tongue without you even thinking about it. It should immediately establish your credibility in the market, explain how your product helps people save money and/or improve productivity, and invite your listener to learn more. But remember, you are not selling your product or service at this point; you are merely creating the impact to launch the momentum of the next more detailed discussion or meeting.

- **"Sell the sizzle, not the steak"**

  This is a well worn saying in sales and it really does apply here. You are pitching the benefits of your product, not the features. You are pitching what your product will *taste* like, not what it's called on the label. People generally make their mind up about someone in the first 10 seconds despite what they say, so earn yourself another 10 by creating a memorable elevator pitch that has a real Wow! factor.

- **Create impact and establish credibility**

  Think about what would impress you if the roles were reversed and *you* had asked the question "So, w*hat do you do?*"
  How would you feel if they replied to you *"Oh, I sell software"*? Would that tell you anything apart from the fact that they are not particularly enthusiastic about their chosen career? No, your opening salvo should grab their interest in a matter of seconds.

- **Short and to the point**

  We believe that the following elevator pitch example ticks all the boxes;

  "I'm a Global Account Manager at Sticky Sales. We help companies simplify their sales process so they can make more money".

It's simple, to the point, you're not using jargon, and it actually states that you can help them make more money. Which is all good.

- **Practice makes perfect**

  Your elevator pitch is a critical piece of ammunition. You will be using it all the time; on the phone, in the pub, at parties, as well as in prospect meetings. Revise and edit it until you are totally happy and it doesn't sound forced.

  Think about a rock band on tour. They will play the same song maybe 100 times and each time it has to sound fresh and enthusiastic. Practice so that the words automatically appear without you thinking. Then you can focus on your delivery and personal engagement.

- **Use simple words**

  Assume that your listener knows nothing about you or your company. Keep it simple and jargon free, just as you would in a social situation. There will be plenty of time for jargon if the listener latches on and you move to real engagement.

- **Position your company**

  A single word can help to position the status of your company to your listener. In our example above, we used the word "Global" to imply international coverage and success. The listener will immediately register that you have customers around the world and the means to support them, as well as the fact that you will have achieved notable overseas expansion as your solution has been rolled out. All this from one word.

What other single words can you think of that would convey greater meaning?

- **Body Language**

  We will come to body language later in this guide, but when delivering your elevator pitch, remember to look your listener in the eye and speak a little more slowly whilst pitching your voice slightly lower. This will convey elements of pride and sincerity. Which you possess abundance we hope.

- **Sincerity *is* a good thing**

  Remember the rock band? Each of the 100 times they play that song to different audiences they have to sound fresh and sincere. Remember that every listener is a new audience and your chance to shine.

- **Call to action**

  If your listener shows interest in your pitch, be prepared to follow up quickly. Ask questions and listen to the answers. Always have two or three questions that you can use to move the situation on. As with all questions, make them open; how, who, what, why, where, when; *"how do you manage your customer accounts?"*; *"who do you use for a CRM?"* and so on.

Be complementary and mention one of your USP's; *"where we've seen the greatest take-up of Sticky Sales is…………"* then close; *"when might you be available to take a look for yourself. I'd value your opinion"* or something similar.

Qualification Process

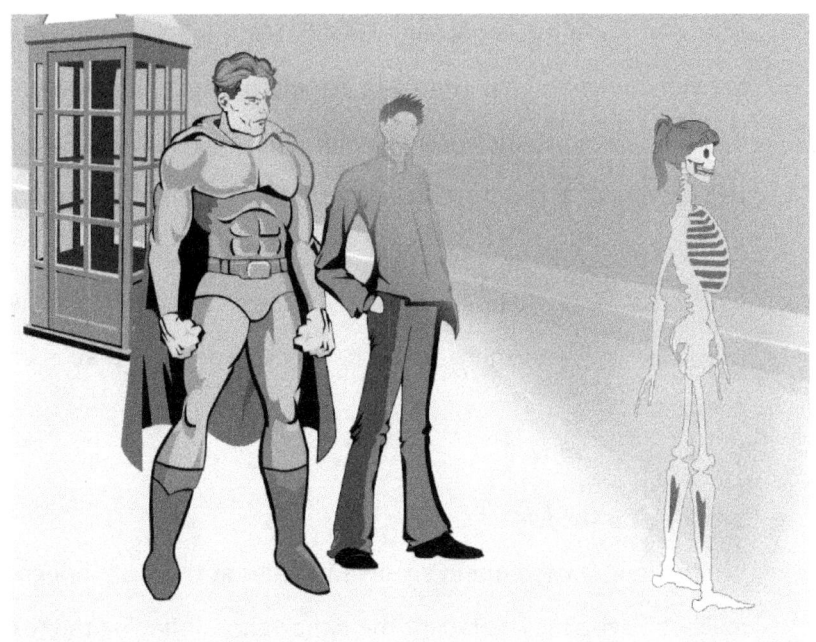

"If only you could see what I'm seeing here!"

SUPER POWER	SUPERHERO	SALES POWER	APPLICATION
Clairvoyance	Dream Girl	**Empathy**	Allow yourself to see the situation as others see it
Object Animation	Giorno Giovanna	**Eloquence**	Concise eloquence brings your product to life
Telepathy	Jean Gray	**Listening**	Listen closely to what your customer is really saying

- **The real stuff**

  So now we get to the real sales stuff. Qualifying your opportunity is one of the most important skills that you must develop if you are not to waste your time and energy on sales that will never happen. This is where you build your pipeline and, harnessing the the powers of a true sales superhero, assess where you're going to make your money this year. Get this right and you'll be happy, your boss will be happy and, most of important of all, your wife will love you even more than she already does (if that is even possible).

- **Working for the MAN.**

  When Steve started out in advertising sales at the Daily Telegraph in Fleet Street, he was taught the importance of finding the **MAN**. He thought this a fine concept, as he could readily accept that we all "worked for the MAN". He had, after all, eagerly viewed many an American TV cop series during his teens; think Starsky and Hutch, Columbo and the classic yet deeply lamentable CHiPs. All of these had characters who either "Worked for the MAN", were prone to declaring "You the MAN" or who, when pressed, would resort to "Stickin' it to the MAN". The MAN was, Steve thought, the perfect illustration of the person with the power; the guy who could make things happen.

- **Money, Authority, Need**

Steve was half way there. MAN was an abbreviation of **M**oney, **A**uthority, and **N**eed.

Money	Make sure he's got the budget
Authority	Make sure he can sign it off (or can tell you who can)
Need	Make sure he needs it

As an introduction to the qualification process this seemed simple. It was common sense surely. And so it proved. Eventually.

- **Quantity or Quality?**

Like all eager young pups, Steve favoured quantity over quality and hit the phones offering ad space to anyone who'd listen. He filled in his call sheets and proudly handed them over to his Manager each evening, subtly pointing out that he literally hadn't stopped all day and she was right this was hard graft this telesales lark wasn't it?

- **Work smart**

With much patience and a little evening wine (this *was* Fleet Street in the last of the good old days) to soothe his exhausted brow, Linda (for that was indeed her name - lovely Linda, who first taught Steve how to sell) explained to him that less is more (see later chapter) and it was all about working smart. Taking time to think about a call before he made it, taking time to do a little research about his target, taking time to find the MAN. If he wasn't talking to the MAN it was a wasted call and a wasted opportunity.

- **Make *effective* calls**

  And that was where Steve was going wrong. He was making 50 calls a day of which maybe 10 were effective, meaning that he had a slightly meaningful conversation with someone, and of that 10 had probably only spoken to one MAN. Steve's colleague Timmy meanwhile, around whom life seemed to waft more languidly than his own, made around 15 calls a day and spoke to 3 MANs (MEN?). From those 3 properly effective calls, Timmy would generally make 1 sale. Which was 1 more than Steve.

  So what was Timmy doing to qualify the opportunity and get the sale?

- **Timmy used open questions**

  It seems obvious but don't ask questions to which the answer could be a straight negative.

"Do you look after your CRM system?"	Answer: *"No"*
"Do you want to talk about how we could help you?"	Answer: *"No"*
"Can I interest you in our services?"	Answer: *"No"*
"Would it be ok if I sent you some information?"	Answer: *"No"*

If you want someone to open up to you, use open questions. Prefix everything with Who, Why, What, Where, When and How.

"Who looks after your CRM system?"	Answer: *"Oh, that's me"*
"What is most important to you when choosing a supplier?"	Answer: *"Someone who is honest, consistent and takes a real interest in me"*
"How would you prioritise what you need?"	Answer: *"We have to make sure that our critical deadlines are met next month"*
"In a perfect world, how would you like it to work?"	Answer: *"I just need a solution that I can trust and not have to micro-manage"*

- **Question, Question, Summarise, Close**

The above are examples around which you should work, using your own products and services. In business as in life, you are trying to get your person to talk about himself. Asking the right sequence of questions, summarising the answers and then closing for the next steps are exactly what you're looking for, i.e;

"So, if we guaranteed that your deadlines are met next month by allocating one of our most experienced project managers, how would that help you?"

Remember, it's mostly common sense, so don't worry too much about the structure. Question. Question. Summarise. Close. There are many formal sales courses out there and we strongly recommend taking at least a few so that you cement effective questioning techniques in your mind, but remember the basic rules and you will be absolutely fine.

Take a look at our list of 25 effective qualification questions, and see how you could apply them to your own products and services.

- **25 effective qualification questions**

   Here are 25 effective qualification questions that will get your prospect talking, convince him that you are genuinely interested in helping him *and* establish your MAN to take you forward in the sale. These should be posed in a conversational style otherwise it's not a meeting, it's an interrogation. And you don't have to use all the questions; just make sure that he's got the Money, Authority and Need.

1. How long have you been here/with your company?
2. How are you organised within your department?
3. What are your biggest challenges?
4. How do/will these challenges affect you?
5. What has changed most about your business in the last 3 years?
6. What do your customers like most about your company?
7. What problems have you been experiencing?
8. How does that affect you financially?
9. What financial considerations are the biggest headache for you?
10. What longer term strategies have you set in place?
11. What are the most exciting opportunities you have coming up?
12. How will you measure if this is successful?
13. What needs to change from where it is today?
14. What would you like to accomplish?
15. How is your competition reacting to what you do?

16. Where does your company have a competitive advantage?

17. If you had a magic wand.......what results would you like to see?

18. What is most important to you, personally, in resolving this issue? Why is that?

19. How would you prioritise what you need?

20. What conditions need to be satisfied for our companies to do business?

21. What budget have you established?

22. What is your time frame?

23. What is most important to you when choosing a supplier?

24. Other than yourself, who else would be involved in the decision to proceed?

25. When can we sit down again to take this forward?

Impact and Momentum

SUPER POWER	SUPERHERO	SALES POWER	APPLICATION
Fire Breathing	Ghost Rider	**Assertiveness**	Use controlled assertion in sensitive situations
Flying	Superman	**Momentum**	Move with purpose, agility and grace; keep your eyes on the prize
Super Speed	The Flash	**Responsiveness**	Respond quickly and effectively to every opportunity

- **Be militarily strategic**

  Sun Tzu, the fabled 6th Century BC Chinese General, Philosopher and Strategist had many observations on how to conduct successful warfare. His treatise, *"The Art of War"*, has been studied by both military tacticians and business people alike. In the section entitled "Every Superhero Needs an Assistant", we will take a look at some of his ideas in more depth, but the principle that we particularly favour is the necessity to create impact and momentum to achieve your objectives.

- **Move them along**

  After seeing your product demo, your prospect may well agree that they are interested but they are not quite ready for a proposal. When you follow-up with them on the agreed date, they are still interested but not yet ready to move forward. They need your help to be moved along or initial enthusiasm will diminish and you will lose the opportunity.

- **What's the hold up?**

  If your prospect is stalling to sign a deal or they keep changing appointments, then you need to find the underlying cause of the problem. It may be that the customer is unsure about something and needs further clarification. It may also be that one of the members of their team has raised a concern that needs addressing. Whatever the situation, if you feel the client is hesitating, get to the bottom of the problem by just asking them:

  "Is there anything that is stopping you from moving ahead with the proposal?"

- **Offer a free workshop**

  You should consider offering the client a free workshop to uncover some of their pain points and to engage with other members of their team who may still need convincing. Your willingness to help will go a long way to securing the deal.

- **Make sure documents are ready**

  Make sure you have your contract, terms and conditions, service level agreements, invoice and any other documents related to the sale prepared in advance. Have these ready and kept up to date at all times. Do whatever you need to do to plug the delay gaps in the process. Delays give the client time to reevaluate their decision so make sure you are prepared.

- **Just ask for the order!**

  Obvious, but it's amazing how few sales people do it. If you sense that your customer is ready, ask for the order. If you are progressing well with the demo and discussions, even a "no" at this stage will mean "not yet".

- **Send "good news" to the client**

  As we've said before, people want to be part of something exciting. Quite often, sending a prospect some good news will encourage them to put pen to paper and sign off a deal. Good news may be in the form of a press release about a new product launch or a success story to which they can relate.

- **Proof of concept**

  If the sale requires a proof of concept, ensure that this happens as quickly as possible. Delays in this area normally mean you either don't have the capacity to implement the solution, or you've "blagged" something in your sales pitch that doesn't exist. The quicker you can prove that your solution meets their expectation, the faster your prospect will sign the order. Get your technical teams in gear.

- **Line up your 3rd parties**

  On occasion, your proposal may be positively influenced by bringing a third party into the equation. If this is the case, make sure you line them up in advance. This third party connection may not be directly involved with your proposal, but the fact that it may help your prospect in other ways can show that you truly care about them.

Every Superhero needs an Assistant!

"Sun Tzu, my old mate. We have work to do!"

SUPER POWER	SUPERHERO	SALES POWER	APPLICATION
Invisibility	Invisible Woman	**Wisdom**	Less is always more; know when to ask for help
Physical Duplication	Naruto Uzumaki	**Teamwork**	Ensure your team is fully briefed and supportive
X-Ray Vision	Superman	**Observation**	Observe people and their habits; you will adapt yourself

- **Get an assistant!**

  Even a superhero needs a little help from his assistants from time to time. Superman has Lois Lane, Spiderman has Mary Jane, and you, my budding little Sales Superhero, have Sun Tzu the Chinese General, Philosopher and Military Strategist from the 6th Century BC, whose treatise "The Art of War" has been studied and adapted over the last 2,500 years by successful generals, business leaders and yes, sales people.

  Now admittedly, Teri Hatcher and Kirsten Dunst may appeal more as your assistant, but you will learn how helpful our dusty old General can be in your heroic endeavours.

  Here, we look at a selection of quotations from the great man, and how they are relevant to effective sales techniques.

- **Sun Tzu and the Art of Sales**

  "Now the general who wins a battle makes many calculations in his headquarters before he fights a battle. The general who loses a battle makes but few calculations beforehand. Thus do many calculations lead to victory and few calculations to defeat. Hence, to fight and win in all your battles is not the foremost excellence; to break the enemy's resistance without fighting is the foremost excellence."

It's our old friend, the Six P's – Perfect Preparation Prevents Piss Poor Performance.

- **Pick your battles**

  "He who knows when to fight and when not to fight will win."

  Be honest with yourself and only go for the sales that you think you will win. You will save an enormous amount of time, your forecasts will be more accurate, and you will make more money. Your manager will also be happier and confident to leave you alone to concentrate on your pipeline.

- **Be adaptable**

  "He who knows how to handle both superior and inferior forces will win."

  The essence of being a true sales superhero. You must understand when and how to apply your techniques according to the sales requirement and situation. One size does not fit all. This is also a useful tip to remember when managing colleagues at all levels within your own organisation.

- **Get your team behind you**

  "He whose army is united in purpose throughout all its ranks will win."

Make sure that your team is fully briefed and has absolute understanding of what is required of them throughout the sales process. You're a talented sales superhero and will reap the rewards, but it is a team effort.

- **Do something different**

  "He who prepares himself and waits to take the enemy unprepared will win."

  Choose your moment and outsmart your competitors. This will only be achieved by maintaining a thorough knowledge of your prospect and his buying cycle. By anticipating potential pain points, you will be ready to strike before your prospect reaches out to the general market.

- **Know when to bring in the big guns**

  "He who has military capacity and is not interfered with by the sovereign will win."

  Your senior executives are there to support you and should always have your best interests in mind, making sure that you are properly equipped to offer an effective, professional service to your customers. But you should use your managers wisely. Just as you don't have to bore them with every intricacy, gossip and rumour about the opportunity (and nor will they be interested), you should assess the right time to bring them in as *"corporate heavyweights"* to assure the prospect of your commitment to them, and to outline future strategies. Less is definitely more though.

- **Plan and practice**

  "He wins his battles by making no mistakes. Making no mistakes brings certain victory, for it means conquering an enemy that is already defeated."

  Ensure that you are fully prepared for every meeting and know your objective at each stage of the sales process. Be confident to engender the trust of your prospect and, after the initial impact, maintain momentum so that your competitor will find it difficult to catch up with you.

- **Use all your resources**

  "In all fighting, use the direct method for joining battle and the indirect method to secure victory."

  You are the point man and facilitator for your customer. But you should always *"surround"* your customer and employ all your company's resources to move towards sales closure. This means briefing your team; marketing, engineers, administration, management, etc. about everything that is required to win the deal. Have your colleagues reach out to people that they know within your customer's organisation, even if they have nothing to do with the specific requirement or decision. You are trying to encourage positive noises that will filter to your MAN and his stakeholders. This may appear to be time-consuming but it does work, and your colleagues are only keeping in touch with people they already know.

- **Own the relationship**
  "Whoever is first on the field and awaits the arrival of his enemy will be fresh for the fight; whoever is second on the field and must hasten into battle will arrive exhausted."

Make your customer your new best friend. Your relationship with him is vital to any future success. You will anticipate and uncover pain points and requirements before your competitor even gets a hint, and your professional response will be with your customer while your competition is scrambling to provide a solution.

- **Concentrate on the pain points**
  "You may advance and be absolutely irresistible if you attack the enemy's weak points; you may retire safely from all pursuit if you move more rapidly than the enemy."

There is a military concept derived from Sun Tzu, that you should mobilise your full strength against an enemy's weak points, and avoid those that are strong. In other words; *reinforce strength and starve failure*. Of course, your customer is not your enemy; that accolade is reserved for your competitor. However, once you have uncovered your customer's pain point, brief your team and focus all your resources on providing a rapid and effective solution. Again, it's all about impact and momentum.

- **Manoeuvre yourself**

"He will conquer who has learnt the art of deviation. Such is the art of manoeuvring."

This is not a blanket instruction to be devious. But as a sales superhero, you will be naturally adept at people-watching and be sensitive to relationships and situations. You must be ready to manoeuvre swiftly and silently within this environment. Some of the best sales people we have worked with have developed what we call *"silent assassin"* mode. You never saw them coming.

- **A problem is an opportunity**

"If, in the midst of difficulties, we are always ready to seize an advantage, we may extricate ourselves from an unfavourable situation."

Sad to relate, but it is inevitable that problems will sometimes arise. Late delivery, incorrect invoicing or operational personality clash are examples of issues that can be outside of your control or influence. If something like this does occur, you should move quickly and decisively to correct the problem, and implement a new structure to ensure non-repetition. This will cement your position as your customer's go-to-guy and instil even greater confidence in your abilities to help him fix his pain points.

- **Keep your friends close, but your enemies closer**

   "Now victory may be produced for your army from the tactics used by the enemy, though they as the multitude cannot comprehend how victory was actually achieved."

   You should know your competitors' sales people and even socialise with them when appropriate; industry drinks evenings for example. By talking to them and maintaining confidentiality, you will learn their style and attitude and form an understanding of how they work. A healthy respect for each other is admirable, but remember that they are your competitor and want to take money away from your children. As you become more adept at managing these competitive relationships, you will even learn to drop subtle smokescreens and deviations, but these should be used sparingly otherwise all perceived trust is lost.

   In our opinion, a bonus of the role and one of the most enjoyable extra-curricular activities to be had, is the shadow-sparring, probing and deception that goes on over an evening drink, but don't forget that they are doing it too! However, with humour and the mutual knowledge that everyone is looking for leads and advantage, you may even make a real friend or two.

We'd like a Presentation

"To be a presenter or not to be a presenter. <u>That</u> is the question"

SUPER POWER	SUPERHERO	SALES POWER	APPLICATION
Clairvoyance	Dream Girl	**Empathy**	Allow yourself to see the situation as others see it
Materialisation	Green Lantern	**Preparation**	Be mentally prepared and have all your tools to hand
Time and Space Manipulation	Hiro Nakamura	**Control**	Don't rush the process; give people time to absorb things

- **Presentation means presentation**

  The *Less is More* principle very much applies when giving a presentation to your prospect or an existing customer. You are there to *present*, not to relate the history of technology since the Babbage Difference Engine. You've worked hard for this moment so stick to the brief.

- **Presentation skills are important**

  Although the frequency of the formal stand-up slide presentation has undoubtedly reduced in recent years, there are many extremely useful aspects that you should master, and there will *always* be occasions when you will have to formally present. The key to this is Preparation, Rehearsal and Tell, Show, Tell.

- **Tell Show Tell**

  Generally, people like structure. They feel safer that way. They like to see a beginning, a middle, and an end. So you must tell them what they're going to see, show it to them, then tell them what they've just seen. Think of any successful TV programme; Strictly, Top Gear, Bake Off, The Apprentice, Dragon's Den, whatever (we like The One Show but what are you going to do?)

- **Tell (Agenda and Objective)**

  The programme starts. You're assailed by punchy music and shiny visuals. Tess, Jeremy (possibly), Mel & Sue, Voiceover Man or Evan tell you what a great show they have for you this evening.

Brief snippets of delight are displayed to tease your interest. Impact is created.

- **Show (Content and Momentum)**

  The show moves into content phase. Detail is shown. Tension is built. You are brought into the fold as the presenter continues to keep you interested by telling you what's coming up next. You are being led to a conclusion. You can't help yourself but want to see the outcome. Momentum is achieved.

- **Tell (Summary and Close)**

  The show ends and your breathless presenter tells you what you've just seen and what a great show it was. You tacitly agree that, because you have invested your valuable time in it, it has indeed been a fine show. You are shown highlights and implored to return next week for what promises to be even better. You hit the Series Record button and closure has been made.

- **Enjoy the presentation**

  We all know that one of the major fears in life for many people is public speaking. This is perfectly understandable, and most people will not have to do it. But *you* are a sales superhero and you *have* to do it. So you may as well try and enjoy the experience. And the route to the enjoyment and reducing much of the fear is in preparation and practice, like most things in life. Only by working at this will you achieve control; and by achieving a measure of control you will reduce your levels of stress, because stress is a manifestation of feeling that you are *not* in control.

- **Your audience want you to succeed**

  Your audience will instinctively support you and want you to present well. They are attending your presentation because it is important to them and they are investing their valuable time in you.

- **Isolate the clever dick**

  If you have a clever dick in your audience who wants to prove he knows more than you, or is eager to impress his colleagues (it happens), you should acknowledge that person immediately and thank him for his contribution. Then, address the whole group and assure them that you have allotted plenty of time for questions following the presentation. This means that you maintain control and effectively isolate and remove any frequent interruptions.

- **Be passionate**

  Obviously, don't overdo it, but your audience should see that you are proud of your product, and you truly believe that it will fix their pain point. Using power words such as *"believe"* rather than *"think"*, *"value"* rather than *"price"*, *"because"* rather than *"as"* will, when combined with your confident attitude, convey a sense of permanency in your audience's minds. Other powerful and persuasive words include;

  - You
  - Money
  - Save
  - New
  - Results
  - Easy
  - Health
  - Safety
  - Love
  - Discover
  - Proven
  - Guarantee

- **Dry presentations will turn to dust**

  There really is nothing worse than sitting through a presentation that consists of line after line of text on interminable slides that are being dutifully read verbatim to you by a bored presenter in a flat monotone voice who would clearly rather be anywhere but here and is using too many bullet points in too small a typeface in the wrong shade of grey....*sigh*!

Make your presentations enjoyable and people will remember them. Include pictures, charts, video, music (all simple insertions these days), ask questions, involve your audience, be self-effacing, and use gentle humour. You will be more relaxed, and your audience will relax with you.

- **Start well**

  Your opening remarks will settle you *and* your audience so make them count. Smile and thank them for being there. We like to say something like:

  "Thank you for coming along today. We know you're busy people but we have 97 slides to get through, so let's get started".

  Pause for effect, usually laughter, and then reassure them that it's a lot shorter, and take them through the areas that you will cover (the agenda). And you're off, everyone more relaxed than just 30 seconds before.

- **Close early**

  After talking your audience through the presentation areas (agenda) you should get in an early soft close. For example:

"So, as you can see, by the end of this session you will have a clear understanding of how our solution will address your <u>insert customer's pain point</u>".

- **Start on time**

  Start your presentation on time even if some of your audience is late (unless it's your main sponsor). You will lose elements of control and respect if you display indecisiveness at the outset.

- **Attention span is limited**

  People retain around 70% of what they hear, compared to 10% of what they read (the other 20% is reserved for touch, which is probably not advisable in a professional environment).

  You should use no more than 5 bullet points per page and not read directly from them. Think of bullet points as an aide-memoire for you to impart interesting examples, stories and applications of your product.

  Try to make your presentation last no longer than 30 minutes at most. It should be a reference point to prove, provoke or pre-empt your customer's requirement. It is not an end in itself.

- **Customise your presentation**

  You may be tempted to use standard templates or the presentation that worked well for you the last time. Don't. Both you and the presentation need to be fresh. Tailor your slides to each requirement and try not to merely trot out the corporate overview.

- **Be imaginative**

You want your audience to remember you over your competitors. Modern presentation software allows you to insert all manner of audio, images and video. Use them sparingly and in context. Is there a piece of music that could be playing over your cover slide as your audience arrives and again as they leave?

Over the years, we have variously used (when appropriate);

- In the City (The Eagles)
- I Feel Good (James Brown)
- Help (The Beatles)
- Theme from Mission Impossible (Larry Mullen & Adam Clayton)
- It's a Burden being Wonderful Like Me (Steel Panther)

There is always a song that will apply but think carefully about your audience and when to use it. When used with humour, music can be a powerful tool.

- **Be a little bit cheeky**

  Many people will attend a presentation with the preconception that it will be dry, non-inclusive and, not to put too fine a point on it, boring. Try to address this by having an ever so slightly subversive cover page on screen as your audience arrives (possibly with background music).

  An example that worked very well for us some years ago was a presentation to the IT team at a large investment bank who were preparing to relocate to larger premises in the City of London. We wanted something a little different and amusing for our cover page, so we contacted the appointed firm of architects working on the new building, and managed to obtain one of those "artist impression" pictures of the new location.

  Over this, we superimposed a picture of delivery vans and a double decker bus in the street outside. We then applied our company logo onto every van and a company tagline onto the bus. We said nothing as our audience arrived for the presentation, but the smiles and whispers as people noticed the slide got everything off to a very good start.

Writing a Compelling Response

"Now this could be a big order!"

SUPER POWER	SUPERHERO	SALES POWER	APPLICATION
Memory Manipulation	Professor X	**Knowledge**	Know your product, facts, figures and USP's
Object Animation	Giorno Giovanna	**Eloquence**	Write with concise eloquence to empower your product
Web Spinning	Spiderman	**Solutions**	Describe the benefits of your product to your customer

- **Drumroll please! They've invited us to respond!**

  During your time as a Sales Superhero you will have many opportunities to display your eloquence and creative writing skills. As a result of your expert prospecting and lead generation, you will eventually reach the nirvana that is an invitation from your client or prospect to respond to an RFI, RFP or RFQ.

  This is a very good thing indeed as it has rewarded your efforts in encouraging the prospect to take you seriously. You can pat yourself on the back and congratulate yourself on a job well done.

  However, the job is not even half complete and writing a compelling response can be fraught with serious considerations. Despite your understandable excitement at being invited to bid or respond, there are a few critical points to consider before you fire up your templates:

  1) Should your company respond?
  2) Can you win this opportunity?
  3) Can you meet the deadlines?

  It is always tempting to respond to everything in the hope that something will stick. But this is time-consuming and will sap your energy as you labour late into the night over an opportunity that you are clearly not going to win. As any good superhero knows;

you choose the field of battle that is most advantageous to you, and then only fight the battles that you can win.

- **It's okay to decline**

  A polite note of decline and retreat to fight another day will always be more respected by your customer that the alternative; a mash-up of a response that has been hurriedly pasted together from unrelated templates and collateral. Remember, if your response has not had a little thought and heart behind it, then it will appear just so, and you run the very real risk of insulting your customer.

  However, having decided that the instance *is* an ideal opportunity for you to pitch the superiority of your products and services, and that you wish to co-ordinate your team to create an attractive and compelling response, the next steps should be carefully planned.

- **RFI (Request for Information)**

  A request for information is exactly what it says. This may be issued direct from the customer or their appointed team of consultants to identify what is out there, market trends, and to establish the prime service providers for their future RFP. Your response will not result in a contract at this stage, but will enable you to position yourself as a leading contender for the business. The RFI is an opportunity to influence the content and expectations of the RFP, and allows you to establish your credentials within the industry.

- **RFP (Request for Proposal)**

  A request for proposal (or tender) on the other hand, can be a major exercise and a resource-intensive and time-consuming proposition. An RFP is often prepared and issued by your customer's Procurement team against your end-users' technical criteria, and will be aimed at getting the best commercial deal for the company.

  RFPs have a habit of popping up at the last minute which can result in a frantic scramble to respond within the deadlines provided.

  A lot of tender requests can be in a loose, unstructured format, due to the Procurement team's lack of knowledge in the technical requirement. This leads to repetition and inconsistencies in the requests. In responding, you are usually given the opportunity to request clarification on any point, so it is vital that you read the request carefully.

- **RFQ (Request for Quotation)**

  A request for quotation is used for more common off-the-shelf products with set specifications that are readily available in the market place. The customer will use this document to compare pricing for a specific product across many or several vendors, and look to settle upon the lowest offer price. Service is not necessarily a consideration as this is a standard plug and play requirement.

- **Open with a punchy Executive Summary**

  It is widely believed in experienced sales circles that upon receiving your RFP response, the production of which has caused you to sweat, curse, weep and purchase new spectacles, your customer calmly turns to the Executive Summary at the beginning, then the Pricing Schedule at the end, and reads nothing in between.

  This may not necessarily be true, but it serves to emphasise the importance of the Executive Summary. Think of it as if it is the only text that your customer will read, and structure it accordingly.

  Remember our elevator pitch? It's an extended version of that. Think impact, credibility and state how you will fix the pain, not a lengthy tome on your company background. Keep it short, no more than one A4 page, and powerful. Again, imagine that your prospect will only be reading this section; what does he want to see?

- **Be fully compliant**

All RFP responses will be marked against evaluation criteria or a scoring system. You will lose points if you state that you are non-compliant to a stated requirement. Also, if there are many responses from many vendors you could even be disqualified on this marking alone. In our view, if you have been included in the bidders list then you are already compliant in some way so ensure that you word your statements accordingly.

- **Use your prospect's terminology**

  You will be tempted to use your own language and possibly your own standard templates in your response. Don't. Every RFP response should be totally customised to the particular customer and requirement. The scoring system may also involve a matching of keywords and phrases that the customer has included in the RFP, so ensure that your written answers include these also. Think of it as the written equivalent of Mirroring (see section on Body Language).

- **Back up your answers with facts**

  Make sure that all elements of your response are backed up with real facts, rather than fanciful wishy-washy phrases that are open to interpretation. Use power word sentence links such as *because* and *which means that* to emphasise and solidify your statements.

- **Take pride in your document**

  There is no excuse whatsoever for submitting a sloppy document full of spelling mistakes, grammatical errors, variations in typeface and disparate headings. It's a constant source of amazement to us that we still see documents containing one or more of these distinctly unprofessional errors pop up today.

  - You will have a company style; use it
  - You will have a standard heading and body text format; use it
  - You have a spellchecker; use it

  We do not doubt your abilities as an all-round sales superhero, but if *you're* not fluent and exact in your written responses, then find someone who is.

- **It's all about the customer**

  Although the RFP is an invitation for you to respond with an offer, it is not all about you. The customer's priority is solving his pain-point (naturally). Just as you wouldn't, or shouldn't, keep talking about yourself in a face-to-face situation if you want to build a rewarding relationship, the same applies in the written sense.

  Look at what you've written and make sure that everything is directed at your prospect's requirement. Start sentences with *You will...* rather than *We will...*

When describing your product, put it into your prospect's context and state how it will fix their pain point and save them money.

- **Never miss the deadline. Ever.**

  You are the person responsible for the bid response. When you receive the RFP, pull your team together to apportion section responsibility. Then agree the deadline for each response back to you. The time will slip away. It always does. Build in at least 2 days for formatting the final document. Just don't miss the deadline.

Proof of Concepts

"Can I try these on for a couple of days?"

SUPER POWER	SUPERHERO	SALES POWER	APPLICATION
Materialisation	Green Lantern	Preparation	Be prepared and have all your tools to hand
Physical Duplication	Naruto Uzumaki	Teamwork	Ensure your team is fully briefed and supportive
Time and Space Manipulation	Hiro Nakamura	Control	Don't rush the process and make sure you have control

- **Blood, sweat and tears**

  Every business has two parts. You already have a lot of blood, sweat and tears poured into developing a new technology. Then, you have to sell it. But selling new technology is often easier than it sounds. You need a way to change how customers think about technology and convince them to embrace your new product.

  Installing a proof of concept at a customer site is a tool commonly used to remove obstacles to the sales process, and help the customer gain the confidence he needs to buy the product.

  Over the years, we have demonstrated consistent success with proof of concepts in a variety of technologies such as SaaS (Software as a Service), solutions to manage data-centres, and project management applications. The key to this success is to incorporate the following tips into every proof of concept.

- **Understand the Goals**

  There are two ways to look at the goals associated with any proof of concept. Your goals are to educate the customer and eliminate any objections associated with your solution that might block a sale. The customer needs to determine two things.

  First, your product has to prove that it can deliver the savings that your sales pitch promised.

Second, you have to demonstrate that your product works in a manner that meets their operational guidelines.

- **Roll in a product evangelist**

  We said earlier in this guide that excitement sells. If you allow someone who does not believe in the product to carry out a POC, their aura will flunk the sale. Enthusiastic people learn every angle of the solution and are far better at presenting than anyone else. You may be surprised to learn that that individual may come often from IT, rather than Sales.

- **Limit the scope of the POC**

  Don't try and prove that your solution can do everything. The customer is only interested in their pain point so tackle that in the POC. Be prepared to show other elements but only if the customer brings them up. Otherwise, narrow the POC to the exact requirements of the customer.

- **Develop a standard routine**

  When you get in front of your customer, you will only have a few hours to impart as much information as you can. You need to develop a demonstration and training routine that will quickly educate them and answer the most common questions. This routine needs to be more than just a training course.

  This is your opportunity to tell your customers how you want them to use your solution and drop deliberate hints about the functionality that you want them to see. When the time comes to deliver this presentation, you do not want to sound like you are reading from cue cards. You need to come across naturally. It should sound relaxed, like you are having a casual conversation. This will help to get your customers talking with you when you are on-site.

- **Understand the customer's environment**

  You need to demonstrate to the customer how you are going to use or replicate these components in your proof of concept. Get all the details you can. Do not assume they are using standard components. You need as much background information as possible to ensure that you know how to work with these components before you arrive on-site.

  Many people forget that the customer's environment is much more than software and servers. It is also people. Proof of concepts are often implemented whilst working with the business owners. You need to identify who you will need to work with, and who needs to be present when you arrive on-site to install the POC.

- **Check client facilities**

  Before you visit the customer, you need to schedule a call with him. The goal is simply to determine if your customer has everything in place that they promised. Is the hardware you asked for ready? Are all the people you require to perform your installation going to be available? If everything is not in place, then you can judge whether to get on the plane, train or automobile and make it work, or whether you need to reschedule.

- **Spend quality time with the customer**

  Most proof of concept installations that we have implemented over the years took about half a day to complete. Spend the rest of the time talking to the customer and digging more on their problems and how you can address them. Once you've completed the POC, assuming it has been successful, the likelihood is that your customer will be asking all sorts of questions.

  The fact is that the moment you step out of their building they'll be too involved with their day-to-day tasks to bother touching the hard work behind your POC. So the best thing is to:

  a) Drive the customer and get them to commit to follow-up dates
  b) Agree on an action plan for the next session

- **Follow up call**

You should set an expectation that you will be giving them a call within 3-5 business days. But this really does depend on region. For example, we have found that the Middle East, North Africa (MENA) region tends to take much longer when testing a POC compared to Europe.

During the call, you must determine any issues that they have in using the proof of concept. Many of these can be resolved over the phone. Often during these calls, you can identify some of their early concerns. Keep in mind that they probably haven't read the manual, so your customer can still have many misconceptions because they are trying to learn about your product by stumbling across features on an ad-hoc basis.

- **Define next steps**

  The last thing you need to do is close the loop on your proof of concept and begin working with your customer to complete their product evaluation.

  First, you need to make sure that you have completed all the tasks needed to meet the expectation that your POC would be successful. Then, you want to address actively all the technological objections that will affect the product evaluation.

Handling Objections

"£20 for a Martini! You're having a laugh!"

SUPER POWER	SUPERHERO	SALES POWER	APPLICATION
Clairvoyance	Dream Girl	**Empathy**	Allow yourself to see the situation as others see it
Ice Manipulation	Iceman	**Calm**	Maintain your cool at all times; welcome objections
Telepathy	Jean Gray	**Listening**	Listen closely to what your customer is really saying

- **Objections are to be welcomed**

  Let's get this on the table straight away; objections are a good thing.

  That's right. *Objections are a **good** thing.*

  We are so conditioned to react to someone objecting to us, or more commonly something we've said, in everyday life, that we automatically retreat into one the following modes;

a.	Defensive
b.	Hostile
c.	Argumentative
d.	Dismissive

  Clearly, any one or combination of these reactions is not going to be conducive to your heroic efforts to close the sale. But you should be softly encouraging objections so that once they are addressed and removed, your customer will be certain in his decision to go with you. If there are no objections, then embrace the fact and just close the bloody thing!

- **Qualify the objection**

  If and when your customer raises an objection, you must qualify it immediately. This will give you the time and opportunity to open the discussion and assess whether the stated objection is what concerns your customer.

Respond with:

"What makes you say that?"

This will allow your customer to elaborate upon his concern and give you more information with which to handle the objection and close it off. Interestingly, it also places a microscopic seed of doubt about the validity of his objection in the customer's mind, because you have expressed mild surprise at his question.

This is a very subtle, sensitive indication so you must be confident in your abilities to read the situation, and to use the correct body language.

- **Try not to re-sell**
  An objection is often just a request for clarification, so don't be tempted to sell your product all over again. You should ask your customer why that is so and elaborate upon his concern.

Respond with something like:

"I understand why that could be a concern for you. Could you tell me more about why that's the case and what's most important to you?"

- **Don't be confrontational**

  Of course, you should never argue with your customer. He is fully entitled to raise his concerns just as you are fully entitled to address them. Modern selling is all about working in consultation with your customer to achieve a common goal. Don't fight them and remember the golden rule in any relationship; the first to anger loses.

- **Get them all out there**

  A sales person will naturally wish to conclude the sale after answering an objection. One of the old techniques was to respond to an objection with something like:

  "If can prove to you that is not the case, would you be happy to proceed with the order?"

  But this method *(the Sharp Angle Close)* is considered by some to be a little old hat and confrontational, as it is applying pressure on the customer to commit.

  It is far better to acknowledge the objection, ask your customer to elaborate (*"What makes you say that?"*) and respond professionally. You should then flush out any further objections by asking if there are any other elements that are worrying the customer. If you don't get them out there, they will come back to bite you later.

- **Write it down**

  You must demonstrate your respect and acknowledge the real nature of the objection. Make sure you write the objection(s) down in your notebook and deal with them individually as they arise. When you are sure that there are no more objections to come, verbally summarise the list and your responses back to your customer and move for a firm close, something like:

  "Now that we've cleared up any concerns you may have had, are you in a position to go ahead?"

  If you have judged your relationship and the situation correctly, your customer should be happy to progress. If he still procrastinates, then you should counter with something like:

  "What is the one thing that is preventing you from placing this order? Let's clear that up now so we're both happy to move on".

- **Common sense rules all**

  Be cool and treat objection handling as a joint attempt to find a reason to proceed. Don't try to be too clever with your response. You're a grown adult with good manners and highly developed intuition. Otherwise you wouldn't be doing this job. Use your common sense and adopt a position where your whole persona signifies *"how can we solve this together"*. You will be surprised how effective this small shift in attitude can be.

- **It's too expensive**

  Assuming that you ticked all the technical and operational boxes, the most common objection will be *Price*. Unless he is just being a bit of a twonk (in which case you may want to reassess your target accounts) your customer is not being awkward, but must demonstrate to his business that he has negotiated the very best price and/or cost savings. In the modern business environment, this is how he will earn *his* bonus, by hitting his Key Performance Indicators (KPI's) on a regular quarterly basis.

  However, you should be proud of your price and stand firm. The alternative is to devalue your own product, one that has been set at a fair market price based on years of experience and expertise in your sector.

  Also, by offering an immediate discount, your customer will get the impression that you were asking too high a price in the first place, and a measure of trust can be lost. You are also taking money away from your children by reducing your commission potential.

  You should address the price objection immediately but provide a get-out/face-save for your customer in the form of maintenance credit days (2 days per quarter for example) or priority response guarantees (2 hour instead of 4 hour on Fridays and Mondays), or something similar that is easy to implement and has a low cost to you.

So let's look at some of your options in response to the wonderful thing that is the price objection.

He says *"It's too expensive..."* You say;

- *"Compared to what?"*

- *"Why do you say that?"*

- *"Did we miss something?"*

- *"How much will it cost you to do nothing?"*

- *"Is price the only thing that prevents you signing?"*

- *"Okay, so if the price wasn't an issue, are you satisfied that this is the right product for you?"*

- *"Okay, so which part/element don't you want?"*

All of these responses are designed to reinforce the value of your product to your customer, flush out any hidden objections and for him to understand that a reduced price means a reduced product or service. Help him along with this – he has to ask after all – and he will then be able to justify his decision internally.

- **Say nothing**

A tricky one this, but it can work if you've developed an exceptional relationship with your customer. If you have bonded professionally and socially (within reason) during the sales process, you can sometimes use what we call the Roger Moore response i.e. total silence, raised eyebrow, hint of a quizzical smile. When we've tried this it has absolutely worked, with our customer eventually breaking the silence and saying something like:

"Anyway, let's just get this going shall we?"

It's not for the faint-hearted but a beautiful thing when it comes off.

Closing the Sale

SUPER POWER	SUPERHERO	SALES POWER	APPLICATION
Fire Breathing	Ghost Rider	**Assertiveness**	Use controlled assertion to drive the situation
Flying	Superman	**Momentum**	Move with purpose, grace and expert timing
Super Speed	The Flash	**Responsiveness**	Recognise the opportunity and close the sale

- **Be a natural closer**

    Have you ever met a seasoned salesperson who is just a "natural" at it? Some people seem to have that air of confidence when it comes to sales skills, inspiring awe and envy among those of us who witness their approach to selling.

    These individuals have a certain confidence that shines through, particularly when closing a sale. For the seasoned sales superhero, the close is never overtly adversarial, nor is it pushy. The expert salesperson knows that the close is the heart of the sale. Without this essential last step a sale is not a sale (also remember that it's not a sale until it's been paid for!)

- **Remember to ask for the order**

    This may seem blindingly obvious, but it is something that often goes overlooked. *You have to ask for the order*. Asking for the order can be especially nerve-wracking if you have faced repeat objections or other challenges in earlier parts of the sales process.

Hearing a stream of assorted objections can lead you to feel that your prospect is slipping away, but if you have done your job correctly and asked for the order, you will close the sale.

There is also a theory that sales people are resistant to asking for the order as this is a psychological end point in their relationship with the prospect, and if the sale is progressing well, they may lose the traction and goodwill that they have worked hard to create.

- **Close from the beginning**
  Don't do a hard sell; the cut-throat approach alienates many potential customers. Instead, explain your agenda. Tell the prospect exactly what you're selling and how it can benefit their business. Being upfront about your intentions promotes an honest, mutually respectful, and rewarding discussion, paving the way for a smooth close.

  Create an "Action Agenda" (ref: Peter Thomson International) before the meeting. This will clearly set the points of discussion and steer the conversation the way *you* want it to go.

- **Create a sense of urgency**
  One of the best ways to make this happen is to connect your approach to closing a sale to your prospect's needs. Kindly remind them that if they need to achieve their goal, whatever it may be,

your business is the *only* viable option to aid them in their endeavours.

Reconfirm a list of action steps and check with the client that they are in agreement with them. If they are then you know they're pretty much on board. If they hesitate for whatever reason, extract the objection in their mind and deal with it there and then. Don't shy away from creating a deadline. Seeing a deadline can subtly indicate that you don't need their business and that they need to take action if they want you.

- **Follow through quickly**

  If your prospect gives you every indication that they are ready to buy, act quickly to get the deal done and dusted. Have your paperwork ready and make sure that your proposal (or revised proposals) land in your customer's in-box as quickly as possible.

- **Timing is everything**

  Make sure you that are asking the right question at the right time. If you have not fully satisfied the customer's concerns, you should not rush into the close. Getting this right requires you to gauge the situation because timing is everything when it comes to this final stage of the sale. If you are confident that you've responded to all the customer's objections, you do not want to wait too long to ask for the sale. If you leave your prospect hanging for too long, they may develop second thoughts.

- **Pricing should be clear and simple**

  Lack of clarity creates resistance. The key is to be clear about pricing and deliverables so that there are no doubts in your customer's mind. Don't make things ambiguous or try to be clever with hidden costs. That will create problems for you as you get deeper into your relationship. The clearer you are with your pricing structure and deliverables the better your chances are of closing the deal.

- **Suggest specific terms**

  Rather than asking whether your prospect wants to buy, suggest a specific buying scenario and then ask if he agrees to it. For example:

  "We can send a consultant on Tuesday to begin the 3-day scoping. How does that sound?"

  This addresses three separate questions; the level of person assigned for the task, the price (as you've mentioned a consultant), and the time required.

  If your prospect is uncomfortable with any of the specifics; for example, he wants to start on Monday, then he will say so. You've offered him a chance to make decisions about details that would otherwise delay the sale. But be sure you know enough about your customers' needs to make reasonable suggestions, otherwise you'll sound uninformed and pushy.

- **Take the customer out of their office environment**

  You'll often find the best way to close a deal is to take the customer into a less formal environment where they can relax, chill out and be themselves. They'll begin to open up if they trust you and you'll be able to extract information that they may not have been willing to reveal in the office. That information could influence closure of the deal.

- **Prepare some price alternatives**

  The likelihood is that the customer may try to drive you down on price. Prepare some clever alternative ways to engineer the deal that drive a balance between satisfying what your customer wants and what remains profitable for you. If you stick a stake in the ground, you'll only irritate the customer, and they'll see you as being inflexible. Try to avoid driving your fees down, though, you should be proud of your price and what it represents.

  Re-engineering a deal is better than sharpening your pencil. Of course, there will be situations where you will need to do this, but avoid these by using alternative price closures.

- **Gain customer commitment to the timeline**

  The road to hell is paved with good intentions and commitments are not always fulfilled. However, galvanizing the key decision maker(s) to a timeline really does work wonders.

- **15 Sales Closing Techniques**

  Closing the sale means just that. You have reached the stage in the discussions with your prospect at which you believe the matter can be closed or concluded to his (and your own) satisfaction. Assuming that you have qualified the opportunity and successfully presented a solution that will fix his pain point, now is your moment to strike.

  Here we look at the 15 most tried and tested sales closing techniques. But use them wisely; some are riskier than others. Which technique you use depends on your personal relationship and your intuition as to what will work with him individually.

  1) **The Alternative Choice Close**

     "Would you like that to be installed on Friday or Monday?"

  2) **The Apology Close**

     "I'm really sorry. I must have missed something out or not given you the right information, as you still have some doubts. We both know this product is absolutely perfect for you, so it really is all my fault."

  3) **The Assumptive Close**

     "Here, use my pen, I've got the paperwork ready."

  4) **The Balance Sheet Close**

"Let's put together a list of pros-and-cons on whether you should buy the product."

5) **The Cradle to Grave Close**

   "There never seems to be a convenient time to make any decision in life, so let's put this to bed now."

6) **The Direct Close**

   "Are you ready to place your order?"

7) **The Emotive Close**

   "Your business means a great deal to me personally. Can you see us working together in the coming months?"

8) **The Indirect Close**

   "How does that look?"

9) **The Minor Point Close**

   "Would the installation be better for you on Friday? No? Okay, let's keep it scheduled for Monday."

10) **The Negative Assumption Close**

    "Do you see any reason why you wouldn't buy this product?"

11) **The Pressure Close**

    "You will need to make a decision today as the stock is nearly gone."

12) The Puppy Dog Close (Proof of Concept)

"Before you place your order, I'll leave the product with you for a few days."

13) The Selfish Close

"If you place this order with me, I'll make my target."

14) The Sharp Angle Close

"If I can guarantee to install next Monday, do we have a deal?"

15) The Take-Back Close

"Despite our previous discussions to the contrary, you seem to have a slight problem with something. Would you prefer that I just go, and leave you in peace?"

Remember to ask for the Order!

SUPER POWER	SUPERHERO	SALES POWER	APPLICATION
Super Speed	The Flash	**Responsiveness**	Just ask for the bloody thing!

This is the shortest chapter in this guide. And with good reason.

Because it's simple.

Remember to ask for the order!

We have looked at sales closing techniques earlier on, but one of the most common mistakes and infuriating habits in a failing sales superhero is in not asking the customer for the order. It seems strange but this is the most common failure amongst sales teams everywhere. They are sometimes so engrossed in the process that they simply forget, resist or are too frightened to ask.

Whatever the reason, it is worth repeating again and again; *remember to ask for the order*!

Sales and Account Management

Got the Order. Now What?

"Oh boy! I really need to deliver on this project!"

SUPER POWER	SUPERHERO	SALES POWER	APPLICATION
Flying	Superman	**Momentum**	Stay close and in control of handover to operations
Physical Duplication	Naruto Uzumaki	**Teamwork**	Ensure your team is fully briefed and supportive
Super Endurance	Power Man	**Longevity**	You've worked hard to win the customer; don't lose them

- **Consolidate**

  Congratulations, you've got the order. Now what?

  Maintain your professional standards and thank your customer for their business. Then clearly explain what will happen next in terms of logging their requirement with your operations/delivery team, timescales for delivery, project management introductions; everything that will reassure them that they have made the right decision.

- **Put it in writing**

  When you get back to your office, accept your colleague's congratulations with grace and equanimity, invite them all out for a celebratory drink, and then confirm everything that you have agreed with your customer in writing.

- **Stay in touch!**

  One of the biggest customer complaints is that sales people disappear once they've got the deal. This leaves a slightly sour taste with your customer so make sure that you don't get filed under the "*Missing – Presumed Not Interested*" category. Call your customer regularly to keep them up to date with the progress of their order. If they start to chase you for status then you may have a problem.

- **Drive your team**

  It's your head on the block if your support team don't deliver to the specifications that you've agreed with your customer. Once the order is entered into your internal system, call a meeting with your team and brief them on the background, priorities and expectations of the sale or contract. Explain to them that you want **no surprises** and that if there is even the slightest chance of an issue arising, they are to inform you immediately so that you can pre-empt the situation with your customer. Confirm the action points resulting from the meeting by email so that everyone knows what is expected of them.

- **Buying mode**

  Once your product has been successfully delivered and/or installed you are in a very good position indeed and should mobilise accordingly. Your customer has placed his trust in you and it has been rewarded with a positive result. Now is the time to request a further meeting to discuss any future requirements or pain points that you can solve for him. He will be in buying mode, but remember that you are looking for a long-term relationship whereby you are the first person he calls for help, so don't be over eager.

- **Point them in another direction**

  It may appear to be twisted logic, but you can occasionally recommend an alternative or cheaper product from another vendor when you or your company have neither bandwidth nor stock to fulfil an urgent requirement. You must be careful with this, clearly, but your customer will have even greater respect for you as you are tangibly demonstrating your desire to help him at all costs.

- **You work for your customer**

One of the assurances that we have made to our customers over the years is that they should consider us as an extension of their team. We are their representatives within our company and will ensure that they get what they need when they need it.

One of the greatest compliments that was ever paid to Steve was from the Voice Services Director at a major European investment bank. It had been a substantial trading floor requirement that involved network design and integration, as well as a multitude of product demonstrations to IT, Procurement and trading staff. Steve's main competitor held commercial bank and pension accounts with the prospect and it was a complex, hard-fought sale.

Steve was successful, and the contract was awarded to his company. Following installation, Steve invited the Voice Services Director to dinner in the City as a small thank you for his business and, as they refreshed their glasses, asked him exactly why he had won the business. His reply surprised Steve and he was momentarily unsure whether or not to be slightly offended.

"Steve" he said, *"At no stage during the whole process did we feel that we were being sold to. We felt that you and your team were there for us, understood exactly what we were trying to achieve and that you had complete faith in your product. We felt that you were an extension of our team"*.

Steve was not offended despite his initial surprise at being seen as a professional salesman who did not sell to his customer! Steve took his words as an enormous compliment, which of course they were.

You should recognise your place in the grand scheme of things and consider yourself part of your customer's team. That will then become the foundation of your relationship and elicit more business over the years.

Upselling and Cross-Selling

SUPER POWER	SUPERHERO	SALES POWER	APPLICATION
Animal Morphing	Beast Boy	**Adaptability**	Adjust your pitch to create extra value and revenues
Super Speed	The Flash	**Responsiveness**	Be ready to upsell or cross-sell at every opportunity
Time and Space Manipulation	Hiro Nakamura	**Control**	Don't rush the process; stay focused and in control

- **Would you like fries with that?**

  McDonalds' simple counter offer (pun intended) is probably one of the best examples of how successful cross-selling can bring in significant additional revenues and profit, here in the multi-millions of dollars, all around the world. McDonalds have managed to get it just right; the customer is in full buying mode, the additional expense is minimal, but the value to both parties is substantial (who doesn't like a chip?)

- **Get your timing right**

  Only offer additional products or services when your customer has already decided to buy. Striking too early in the sales process will lose focus on the initial product offered.

- **Probe for opportunities**

  You may already have elicited another requirement when discussing your prime product offering, but park it until you have closed the main event. Then quickly bring it in and remind the customer what he has already mentioned would be an additional benefit to him, and offer to roll that product into the sale.

- **Don't be greedy**
Don't get carried away with upselling too much or you will crash your customer's budget on what could be a secondary sale of greater value.

- **The upsell must provide extra value to your customer**
It should not be considered a throw-away item with which to grab more cash or get rid of excess stock. Make sure that your upsell is relevant to the customer, and that it will add real value to his business. If your qualification process has been executed properly, this should fall easily into place.

- **Line up your cross-sell products**
Your cross-sell products should be relevant, useful and offer a lower cost option if bought at that particular moment in time. So, if you have just closed a sale for IP desk phones, for example, say that you have headsets available that you would be willing to bundle into the order. If the customer shows interest just ask how many he wants.

- **Get your marketing ducks in line**
Talk to your manager and marketing team about linking associated product, resources and accessories to your prime product offerings within your company web pages, and encourage

your customer to look at them. This will position the links in their mind and make your cross-sell offer more logical and seamless.

- **Tell them what other people buy**

  You can mention quite innocently and in convivial conversation what other customers sometimes add to their order, and state the benefits that they experienced. Of course, this should only be attempted once you have secured the order for your prime offering, and you have pre-checked that the items or resources are available.

- **Use your notes**

  During the course of your sales process with the customer, you will have asked him lots of questions in an effort to uncover, isolate, and address his pain points. Focus on your prime product offering, but check and scan your notes for other qualified opportunities that can be up or cross-sold.

Track your Sales Progress

"It's all going very well!"

SUPER POWER	SUPERHERO	SALES POWER	APPLICATION
Ice Manipulation	Iceman	**Calm**	Maintain your cool and know where you are against target
Memory Manipulation	Professor X	**Knowledge**	Know where your sales are coming from, and repeat
Super Strength	Incredible Hulk	**Stamina**	A year is a long time in sales; keep pushing until the end

- **Your Manager will measure your performance**

  When a Sales Manager has a member of their sales team who is not performing well, he will usually consider 3 aspects;

  1. They don't know what the job is
  2. They don't know how to do the job
  3. Someone or something is interfering with their desire or ability to do the job

  The Sales Manager should clearly communicate to the salesperson the role and objectives of the job (sell loads), provide continuous training, and ensure that they have the tools and environment to perform the role expected of them.

  After that, it's down to you.

- **Measuring sales progress**

  It is a fact of life that you will be measured. All jobs are, whether you're selling hot cross buns, cars, computers or theatre tickets. Within distinct industries and roles, people will be measured against different criteria such as;

Quantity	your sales and acquisitions
Quality	customer satisfaction and margins achieved
Timeliness	results and reports
Cost effectiveness	achievement against KPI's

All these are important in their own right, but you, my friend, have chosen the path of the sales superhero, so you will ultimately be measured on quantity. Or to be more direct; how much money have you made for the company this month, quarter, half, year?

- **Track yourself**

  We will deal with sales management and forecasting techniques in a future guide, but you should not rely on your Sales Manager or Director to tell you where you are against target. That would be unprofessional if not a little embarrassing. You simply have to know your exact state of progress at any given moment.

  Think of it as running your own business. The targets simply must be met, or you will lose your home and your children will sleep in the gutter in pouring rain with packs of wolves descending upon them and slavering hyenas waiting their turn as vultures circle overhead.

  This is indeed a serious business.

- **Break your target down**

  A simple yet useful trick is to take your annual target figure, the figure that you must achieve to remain in gainful employment, and break it down into manageable chunks to focus your mind.

  Let's say that your target is £500k revenue for the coming year.

£500,000 divided by 12 (months in year)	= £41,666
£41,666 divided by 4 (weeks in month)	= £10,416
£10,416 divided by 5 (days in week)	= £2,083

So, you need to maintain a running average of £2,083.00 per day to achieve your target. I realise that this runs the risk of lapsing into condescension when presenting to a noble sales superhero, but you would be surprised at how few sales people do this one simple thing. Keep a spreadsheet, a sheet of paper, a note on your phone, anything. Just do it. It will enhance your resolve and creativity.

- **Be brutal with yourself**

  Having agreed that your prime use to your organisation is to ring the cash bell, you should be brutal with yourself.

  Think back to your new sales assistant, Sun Tzu. Remember how we should always reinforce success and starve failure? If something isn't working, stop doing it. If a product line isn't selling, don't sell it.

  On a more basic level, if you find that your company isn't a good fit for you, you shouldn't complain about it; you should leave and find one that is. Everyone has free choice and life is too short to spend in an environment where you're not happy. Right?

There's no time to mess around here. You will be judged purely on how much money you are bringing in, no matter how much your role is dressed up as Sales Consultant, Business Development Executive or Account Director.

- **Demand support from your management**
  If you believe that you are not being supported by a colleague or department, or that a product line is not fit for purpose, or that the marketing message is wrong, say so.

  If you believe that your monthly target breakdown, in this instance £41,666, is in danger of slipping behind for reasons beyond your control, say so.

  Demand support from your management and tell them what you need to do your job and hit your targets. They will not be shy about coming to you for answers at your weekly sales meeting if you are falling behind, so pre-empt it all and get what you need when you need it.

- **Plan and churn, plan and churn**
  Tracking your progress is very much about keeping the pipeline full and progressive. You will only get out what you put in. Don't become so immersed in any one sale that will require the majority of your time. The customer must believe that he is your only customer, but you have to know *all* of your customers' buying cycles, timing and pain points to forecast and close properly. You

must be on top of your accounts at all times, or your kids will be developing lycanthropic tendencies from their rain-soaked gutter.

Account Management

SUPER POWER	SUPERHERO	SALES POWER	APPLICATION
Animal Morphing	Beast Boy	Adaptability	Adjust your persona to fit the situation in hand
Teleportation	Nightcrawler	Vision	Think ahead and trust your instincts; usually works
Time and Space Manipulation	Hiro Nakamura	Control	Don't rush anything; stay close and in control

- **Keep the client happy**

  Every sales superhero depends on developing and maintaining relationships with quality clients. After all, it took considerable effort and expense to get to this stage, and the last thing you want to do is screw it all up. Consider what makes customers tick and what makes them return to give you repeat business. Successful account management requires a multifaceted approach that affirms positives while accepting shortcomings along the way.

- **Tailor your work to their needs**

  Don't let any side priorities of your business interfere with the attention you should be giving to your customers. Keep your focus on them so you can maintain long-lasting, productive partnerships. You'll achieve the accolades and other hallmarks of success in time.

- **Determine what your customers really want**

  Get to the heart of your customers' needs by understanding their drivers for success. You'll find your customer has certain targets for the year. Find out what these targets are and steer your proposition to help your client achieve them. You can do this in several ways.

  The first is to ask them directly.

  Secondly, use surveys to fact find.

  Another method is to monitor the client's market drivers and determine how you can support them better. Also, check out their competitors and find out how you can build on their successes and improve your client's competitive advantage.

- **Use technology**

  There are several solutions out there that can support your business, in particular, the information that is relayed to your customers. Map out the value you deliver to your clients and determine how technology can speed things up, make it easier, or simply make information more accessible to the client, via a customer portal for example. Avoid spreadsheets at all costs.

- **Always deliver on promises**

  Clients might not expect you to deliver a proposal by the end of the day, but a promise to deliver one changes the game. Be careful about the deadlines that you create. Clients are usually flexible about terms, but consider them set in stone once you quote them. Deliver what you say you will at the appointed time, whether through a phone call, by email or in person.

  Clients value your services most when you show them that you respect deadlines and fulfil promises.

- **Be honest about shortcomings**

  No company is perfect, but many account managers buckle at the thought of admitting organisational weakness to a client. Tell the truth about why you cannot meet every expectation, and clients will trust you more in the long run. They don't expect a business to be flawless, so a clear approach is best. Take responsibility for any company negatives, as ultimately you represent the firm as a whole.

- **Establish regular account review meetings**

  Ask your client for weekly, monthly and quarterly meetings. The weekly meeting should be with team leaders and your client, and focused on discussing any issues. Monthly meetings are all about service performance and improvement. Quarterly meetings should be with higher level management to discuss strategic objectives and the possibility of greater scope.

- **Promote your brand**

  You need to shout out about your brand so that every person in the business knows who you are. Your on-site team should wear corporate clothing which is smart and pleasing to look at.

- **Cross-train staff**

  Your team should be multi-disciplined and be able to take on several roles. This has a number of benefits. Firstly, it allows you to ramp up staff in a particular area when things get busy. Secondly, if someone is unexpectedly away, there'll always be someone to cover for them.

- **Make the buying process easy**

  We've mentioned this before, but we'll say it again as it's a key point to note. Examine every touch point that your customer has with your business and make sure that the experience with your company is as easy as possible. If there's too much paperwork, or chasing around, then the client will look for easier ways of buying.

- **Avoid backlash from all sides**

  Unless you are dealing with the owner of a business, your client has to report to company higher-ups the same way that you do. Keep everyone in the loop so that surprises don't arise. Inquire about whether your client's superiors know of alterations to the developing deal, and inform your company of progress and changes. Your chances of long-term success are greater when you update each side of the equation frequently.

- **Review client expectations and adjust where necessary**
  You can't consider any account management work complete until you evaluate every aspect of the deal. In the case of longer partnerships, your job is to review client expectations on a regular basis and be certain that their focus holds unchanged. Explicit reassurance is best in these cases. Assumptions may cost you dearly.

- **You are an extension of your customer's team**
  Reassure your customer that you should be considered an extension of his team. You will represent his interests within your company and ensure that anything he needs is directed to the right person or department, with appropriate urgency and a timely response.

More Tips on Improving Your Powers

Effective Communication

SUPER POWER	SUPERHERO	SALES POWER	APPLICATION
Clairvoyance	Dream Girl	**Empathy**	What would you want hear from a service provider?
Super Speed	The Flash	**Responsiveness**	Respond quickly and effectively to everything
Telepathy	Jean Gray	**Listening**	Listen closely to what your customer really wants

- **Communicate effectively**

   We know that's just repeating the title of this chapter, but it's the golden rule. Enough said.

- **Follow up or lose**

   As with most elements of the sales process, it really is just common sense. If you don't follow up someone else will. And you'll lose any credibility that you have previously gained.

- **Be consistent**

   You will have closed your previous meeting or call with your customer by promising to follow up with the next steps. Do this consistently. Not only will your customer learn to trust and rely on you, but you will also reap the benefit of moving your prospects up the value chain in a predictable and trackable manner.

- **Keep it simple**

  It *is* simple so keep it that way. Don't be tempted to stray off subject or introduce extra points because you want to impress. Remember, find the pain point and address it.

- **Know the basics**

  Practice your verbal and written skills. They are the tools of your trade. Read widely and keep up to date with a daily online news service; BBC, SKY etc. If you are unable to express yourself clearly and coherently, people will not know where they stand with you.

- **Think before you speak**

  What is it that you want to convey? Use your empathy and ask yourself *"If I were in his position right now, what would I want to hear?"*

- **The 6 P's**

  Preparation is everything, whether it's for a swift coffee meeting or a full-blown boardroom pitch. Remember, *Perfect Preparation Prevents Piss Poor Performance.*

- **Plan your meetings**

  Distribute an agenda and attach any relevant documents to all participants. Meetings should always start on time. This way, you retain control, and everyone feels comfortable with what is going to be discussed.

- **Encourage discussion**

  While control is necessary, make sure that you bring all attendees into the discussion. At the close of each meeting, go to each person in turn to ask if they have any further comments or questions. This will effectively close the session and enable you to follow up.

- **Summarise and follow up**

  At the end of any meeting, formal or informal, verbally summarise what has been agreed and then confirm in a short, concise email. Detailed minutes are for project meetings. Keep your confirmations brief.

- **Learn from Albert**

  There is a study out there by one Albert Mehrabian, a psychologist, who published a paper in the 1960's under the catchy title *"Inference of Attitudes from Nonverbal Communication in Two Channels"*. You should google it, but Mehrabian's Communication Model (for that is what it is called) talks about how we react to both verbal and non-verbal messages.

  Mehrabian looked at ground-breaking new data and analysed how communication is not just about the right choice of words. It's also about our facial expression, the tone of voice and body language.

A statistic based on this study states that we convey around 90% of any message through subtle means and the remaining 10% only from the actual words. Take a look at the study and you'll see why so many people are misunderstood most of the time!

Body Language

SUPER POWER	SUPERHERO	SALES POWER	APPLICATION
Animal Morphing	Beast Boy	**Adaptability**	Adjust your persona to fit the situation in hand
Super Senses	Beast	**Understanding**	Learn to read people and their emotions
X-Ray Vision	Superman	**Observation**	Observe people and their habits; you will adapt yourself

- **Remove the body language barrier**

  You've worked hard to get that important client meeting. You've refined your slide presentation to be pitch perfect. At critical moments like this, don't let sloppy body language place an invisible, unspoken barrier between you and success.

  "Your gestures, voice tone, rate, and volume can all have a profound effect on the success of your negotiations, job interviews, and sales meetings" says Dr. Carol Kinsey Goman, author of The Silent Language of Leaders: How Body Language Can Help.

  You only have ten seconds to make a first impression and establish credibility, trust, power, status, warmth, and empathy.

- **Be confident**

  Always feel as if they need you rather than you need them. After all, you have a solution that fixes their problem. Being just south of arrogant will work in your favour and ensure that you not only have a productive conversation that moves forward, but you'll achieve more in the time you have with your customer. Acting like a softie will get you nowhere, and you'll be trodden on. So be positive at all times.

- **Open your arms**

  Crossing your arms is a negative signal in cultures everywhere around the world. With your arms crossed, you look defensive and closed, or worse still, that you're ignoring what your conversation partner is saying. Keep your arms open so that you appear to be fully involved. Data shows that you retain 38% less information when your legs and arms are crossed. Open up your arms, and your mind!

- **Smile**

  A purely social smile is just the mouth, but a genuine smile uses the eyes. There is nothing more powerfully addictive than a real smile. It can melt hearts and soothe nerves. It will break the ice and make your customers feel at ease with you. They will gravitate towards you. Smile when you enter a room, when you greet people and when you present.

  A manic, fixed grin is not advisable however, as you will risk your audience disappearing to the lift in an explosive cloud of dust, perhaps leaving just one junior employee quaking in his seat at the back of the room. And it is very likely that he will not have the authority to sign an order.

- **Positive eye contact**

  Making good eye contact can build trust and show that you are engaged and interested. If online, choose to use Skype or a video chat rather than email when you anticipate tensions may be high, and you will boost your chances of positive communication. Studies say that people are less hostile and negative when they look into your eyes. So, use those beautiful baby blues to disarm your opponents. But no staring; you're communicating, not trying to find the entrance to their soul with your x-ray vision.

- **Use fewer gestures**

  Have you ever noticed that when media-trained celebrities are interviewed, they don't fidget or distract with too many gestures? The focus stays on them. Your hands should be taking notes, not conducting an orchestra.

- **Use a lower vocal range and speak slowly and clearly**

  Bring your voice down to an optimal range and speak more slowly. It'll give your brain time to think for a split second and prevent you from blurting out some gibberish. Speaking slower than normal helps your customer to understand and digest what you're saying.

- **Embrace the power of touch**

  Did you know that if you reach out and touch someone, they are more likely to say yes and comply with your request? Touching on the arm creates a human bond within milliseconds, as long as it is done in combination with other honest communication.

  However, be careful not to overdo it. Nadeem has been in a situation where a customer's project manager hugged him tightly every time they met, both at hello and goodbye. Nadeem appreciated the sentiment but started to suspect their intentions.

- **Mirroring**

  You will read a lot of guff about mirroring. This is where you copy your customer's stance, position or movements in order to create a bond. In practice, this is an area fraught with danger. If it is too obvious that you are mirroring, your customer could well be;

  - Offended
  - Uncomfortable
  - About to tonk you on the nose, superhero or not

  Our sense about mirroring is to just let it happen. If you are getting on well with someone it will happen naturally; we all do it instinctively. The next time you are enjoying a chat with a good friend or family member, take a little mental step outside of yourself and look at what you're doing. You will be subtly mirroring gestures in a softer, more amiable way; tilting your head slightly when listening, widening your eyes when describing something, nodding gently to indicate understanding. Be natural. The alternative is to look creepy.

- **Posture**

Bad posture demonstrates to others that you have a lack of confidence and energy. Sit upright and tilt your head slightly when listening. This will indicate full attention and interest in what your customer is saying.

- **Handshakes**

Not too firm, not too weak, and never clammy. A brief confident clasp of hands is necessary to show confidence. It is *not* a trial of strength. One chap, with whom Steve enjoyed what he believed to be a friendly rivalry, once gripped his hand for too hard for slightly too long (he'd had a drink), applying ever increasing pressure until Steve loudly declared, with a smile, that he should let go as he was in imminent danger of embarrassing himself.

- **Invasion of space**

Once you invade a person's personal space, you are demonstrating a clear lack of respect and indifference to them. There is no clear measurement, but you will know if you are too close.

- **Looking at your watch**

This may seem an innocent gesture, but it can be one of the most disrespectful things that you can do to another person, no matter how tempted you are. It is such a powerful rejection at every level that we will give you a five-minute break to think about it (you are permitted to use your watch in this instance) and promise that you will never, ever, be so rude.

- **Be conscious of how you appear**

  Our non-verbal signals are the most powerful communicative signals that we possess. Be aware of how you appear to those around you. Walk tall and walk proud. Be non-threatening but assertive. Be respectful and attentive. But don't work too hard at it, let it come naturally otherwise you run the very real risk of looking awkward.

2 Ears and 1 Mouth

"Of course I'm an excellent listener!"

SUPER POWER	SUPERHERO	SALES POWER	APPLICATION
Invisibility	Invisible Woman	**Wisdom**	Less is always more; know when to keep your counsel
Super Senses	Beast	**Understanding**	Learn to read people and their emotions
Telepathy	Jean Gray	**Listening**	Listen closely to what your customer is really saying

- **Just listen**

  Perhaps the greatest skill that you can ever master in sales, and in life itself, is to just listen. You have 2 ears and 1 mouth for a reason. The ratio is 2 to 1. Keep it that way and you will be more successful and make friends more easily than you ever imagined.

- **People like to talk about themselves**

  No real surprise here but as a sales professional you should be developing a natural tendency to get people talking. With the right prompting and (real) sincerity you will have them talking in no time. And the more they talk to you, the more they will like you.

- **The cocky salesman is dead**

  The age of the cocky salesman is, thankfully, long gone. That old comedy cliché of the smooth-tongued, foot-in-the-door, joke-a-minute, won't-take-no-for-an-answer sales rep has been consigned to the great company Ford Capri in the sky. You are not selling something that people don't want. You are listening and helping them. There is a world of difference.

- **Picking up girls (or boys)**

  Think about how you were when you were young. Let's be honest, your hormones were raging, and it was all very confusing. Girls were these wonderful, unattainable creatures that scared you rigid. Your brain said run-away but your body said don't you dare. And then you're at a party and the girl of your dreams notices you. And you've finally learnt from your previous, admittedly sparse, encounters. You talk to her, about *her*. You ask her questions, about *her*. Gentle, respectful, humorous questions. And you listen, really listen. Lo and behold, what happens? If not an actual girlfriend, you've made a friend. And she's a girl! (Or a boy!)

- **Giving respect**

  Listening to someone means that you are respectful and care about what they have to say. They will thank you for it and trust you the next time you are together. They will know and accept that you understand, care and want to help them, and that is pretty much what we're all looking for in life.

- **Who are your friends?**

  We gravitate towards people who are most like us. Think about who your true friends are and why this is so. True friends ask how you are and then truly *listen* to your answer.

- **Who aren't your friends?**

  Sometimes, due to social grouping or just plain old habit, we continue to spend time with people who have little interest in us, and possibly not our best interests at heart. By listening to what they say, and more importantly what they don't say, you will instinctively know who you can trust and rely on.

A couple of years ago, Steve decided to *"spring-clean"* his social circle and only spend time with people who *really* listened to him; in other words proper friends. The result was dramatic; He was happier because he no longer had to make personal or social allowances for people that had no interest in him, his true friends benefited because he could now spend more meaningful time with them, and he managed to remove a lot of negativity from his environment, perceived or otherwise.

Fine-tuning your ability to bond with the right people on a social level will serve you well in your professional life.

- **Listening and Hearing**

  There is a world of difference between listening and hearing. The former is an art. The latter is something that happens.

- **It's all about empathy**

  When you listen properly, you are putting yourself in the other person's shoes, and forming an outline of what it means to be them. This doesn't happen overnight but with practice, the skill will develop and people will instinctively understand that you care about what they have to say.

- **Be discreet**

  The more that you listen, the more you will hear. Never betray a confidence no matter how much you are tempted. It will always come back to hurt you. A friend once went behind Nadeem's back and said some hurtful things in an effort to secure a role that he had been offered, and that the friend coveted. The person that he spoke to was horrified by his lack of loyalty to Nadeem as a friend and confided in him. Not only did that person lose Nadeem as a friend, he lost the respect of a potential employer as well as a number of mutual acquaintances.

- **Bad stuff**

  As an accomplished listener, you will sometimes have to listen to some unsavoury opinions. Don't get drawn into any contentious areas. And don't tell them how stupid they are or they will never confide in you again. Listen to what you have to, withdraw graciously, and deal with them only when necessary.

- **Learning**

  Nothing that you *say* each day will teach you anything. However, if you *listen*, the lessons will continue every time you leave the house.

- **Poor Listening**

  Recently, Steve was having a quiet pint of good Adnams ale with his wife. At the next table to them were two well-to-do couples. One of the gentlemen was clearly well refreshed and enjoying his pre-dinner gin and tonics just a little too enthusiastically. The four were discussing the recent British general election results, always one of the more dangerous topics (along with religion and football).

The man made his point and asked for his companions' opinion. They had hardly opened their mouths when, each time they tried to speak, he interjected with *"No, listen to me…."* This went on for a while with no other opinion being proffered but his own. The topic moved on to their plans for the next day; something about a choice between Minsmere wildlife reserve and the ruined abbey at Leiston (clearly, we're in Suffolk here). Needless to say, everyone was compelled to listen to our hero's preference.

A little later, Steve was waiting to be served at the bar just behind the man's wife and her female friend. The wife was apologising to her friend, somewhat embarrassed.

"Oh, you know what he's like" said the wife.
"Oh we do. Don't worry, we're used to it" sighed the friend.
"He's always been the same" said the wife, *"never listens to anyone"*.
"Oh well" said the friend, *"any idea what you're doing for your 50th?"*
"Not really" said the wife, *"probably just a quiet meal at home. I don't want a fuss"*.

While this is a pretty extreme example of how not to listen, the episode speaks volumes. The man was tolerated, his wife was embarrassed, the friends were resigned and the idea of a birthday party was;

a) Too much to think about

b) Potential for more embarrassment

c) Risky because of people's response

All this because he wouldn't listen.

Successful Business Relationships

SUPER POWER	SUPERHERO	SALES POWER	APPLICATION
Elasticity	Mr Fantastic	Effort	Stretch yourself; always do more than the competition
Super Endurance	Power Man	Longevity	Never give up, and maintain long-term customers
Super Speed	The Flash	Responsiveness	Respond quickly to every request and meeting

- **Coffee and Making Love**

  There's an excellent analogy that our mentor Peter Thomson uses, referring to business relationships as the inexorable progress from "Coffee to Making Love". When you first meet a partner you take them out for coffee. Over time you slowly build your relationship with them, earning their trust and respect with frequent, sometimes small, commitments, until the day arrives that you are both finally ready to consummate your relationship. Which is a good feeling.

  Imagine one end of the room as "Coffee" and the other as "Making Love". Where most people go wrong is that they try to make love before they've finished the coffee, the inevitable result of which is rejection. You need to work the relationship if you and your customer are going to get satisfaction!

- **Nurture your connections**

  In a professional network, a mix of strong and weak connections is natural and even healthy. However, while many of us are adept at building our networks, we don't spend enough time nurturing them. Think of your LinkedIn connections and Twitter followers for a moment. With how many of those connections have you had limited or no direct contact in the past year?

- **Small voice in a big world**

  While there's some residual connectivity via status updates, remember that it can be difficult to break through the noise of a typical day's 175 million tweets and 140 million LinkedIn users posting status and group updates.

- **Congratulate them**

  When a connection starts a new job, is promoted or changes professions, send a congratulatory note and inquire about the change. Use the opportunity to catch up on other matters and provide an update on your status.

- **Provide Professional Leads**

  When you hear of something interesting, let the appropriate people in your network know about it. Think beyond jobs and referrals to everything from committees, board positions, speaking opportunities, writing assignments, and special projects. Offer to provide an introduction if you're comfortable doing so.

- **Post something**

  Everything is electronic now, except when it's not and then it stands out. To get someone's attention, hand write a note and post it to them. Have you recently read a good book or interesting magazine article that you think a contact would love? Post it to the person with a note expressing why you're sending it.

- **Ask their opinion**

  Your contacts are in your network for a reason, so remember to take advantage of their knowledge and experience. While taking care not to contact people too much, reach out when you have a need and you know your contact will be able to assist. Inquire about other matters during the exchange and thank your contact for helping out.

- **Meet in person**

  Remember to meet local contacts for coffee, drinks or lunch periodically. For remote connections, this may not be possible, but if you do travel, try and meet on the occasions when you're both in the same city.

- **Introductions**

  Chances are, many of your connections could help each other out if only they were connected. When you feel an introduction would be beneficial, and both parties have agreed, introduce two of your connections to each other.

- **Check In**

  Don't have an explicit reason to reach out to a connection? Send a short note to check in and inquire about their professional developments. Provide a brief update about yourself and thank the person for being part of your professional network.

- **Re-introduce yourself**

  The truth is we that connect with so many people on networks like LinkedIn that we often can't remember when or why we connected. Perform periodic network housekeeping and reach out to these contacts, conceding that losing touch is sometimes inevitable, but that you're interested in what's new with them.

- **Know when there's a line to cross**

  Business can be brutal. Sometimes you will win a deal, sometimes you will lose a deal and sometimes there will be an option to win a deal if you do something unethical (or illegal). For our part, we work with people that we like and trust. We don't work with people lacking in ethics or morals.

- **Be emotionally intelligent**

  One of the interesting things that we see in business meetings and networking events is how, in a room full of people, you can successfully exclude others from joining in, sometimes without realising! When people try to monopolise the time of others, it precludes anyone else joining in and this is contrary to good relationship-building. Be sure to check that you are not the one doing the monopolising otherwise, you will become the party bore that no one will want to talk to.

- **Keep your word**

  If you say that you are going to do something you should just do it. This will gradually build peoples' level of trust in you which leads us nicely to the last tip.

- **Ears and mouth**

  It's true you have two ears and one mouth so use them in that proportion. The more you listen, the more you will learn! Ask open questions; show interest; encourage people to talk. Remember the first point about offering something? Well, you are offering to listen to them talk and you will get a LOT in return.

Less is More

SUPER POWER	SUPERHERO	SALES POWER	APPLICATION
Invisibility	Invisible Woman	**Wisdom**	Less is always more; know when to keep your counsel
Object Animation	Giorno Giovanna	**Eloquence**	Concise eloquence brings your product to life
Telepathy	Jean Gray	**Listening**	Listen closely to what your customer is really saying

- **White space sells**

  One of Steve's first sales jobs was selling advertising space in a national newspaper. Over the phone. With a typewriter to take down the copy (this was in the last days of the old traditional hot-metal linotype printing, and ultimately the demise of Fleet Street). Hard but happy work. Steve and his colleagues were young, single, drank a little too much Lambrusco in The Cartoonist after work, and some of them (not Steve, as he was having his mullet trimmed) volunteered as stewards at Live Aid.

  In the office, lessons were learned; Steve was taught how to type, properly, with all his fingers; He was taught the art of rapid copy-writing, taking the salient points and putting them into a structure that had impact, momentum and a call to action; He learned never to set foot in the print room without union permission or the Father of the Chapel would be on him like a stack of newspapers.

But one of the best lessons Steve learned was that *white space sells*. The most effective advertisements, the ads that garnered the most response (these things were tracked by Steve's marketing people, smart Clapham types with names like Tarquin and Jacinta) were those that said the least.

Steve remembers an expensive full-page ad being placed by an agency for their client, a national airline. The page was completely blank, completely white, except for a single 6-point line of text in the centre of the page that said something like:

"We get you there. In comfort. For less".

And beneath the text just their logo and a telephone number. Apparently, the response was dramatic, and bookings went through the roof.

Our eyes are drawn to clear, simple solutions. So are our ears.

- **A quick decision**

We all know that most people have a limited attention span. That's why you normally have about 20 seconds to get someone's attention in verbal form and even less with the written word. We are conditioned as human beings to constantly monitor and assess the factors that are most important to us as an individual. We're no anthropologists, but we would hazard a guess that it's a survival thing. The ability to make a quick decision about the best course of action in the shortest space of time may well have saved lives when a ravenous sabre-toothed tiger hopped into your cave.

- **Get to the point**

  People want a quick fix to their problem. This is why you, as a sales superhero, once you have found their pain point, should address it clearly and concisely. Tell them that you understand their issue, you *feel their pain* (pass the bucket), and that you will make it better.

- **Stick to the brief**

  People want solutions, not War and Peace. If they have one particular problem that you can solve, then make sure that you focus on this completely.

We once attended a "Product Bake-off" where five telecommunications vendors were invited in to present their specific solution to a bank's technological needs. We briefed the vendors beforehand. They fully understood what the customer was looking for and that the requirement was urgent.

Three of the vendors duly chose to present the history, locations and financial structure of their company, the features and benefits of their entire product range and their five-year vision of where the market was going.

The other two vendors, presented their solution to the bank's issue and how quickly it could be installed. It will come as no surprise to you that the latter were invited to bid and the former were not.

- **Address the pain point**

  Don't be tempted to extend the brief unless you are invited to. Address the pain point and the rest will follow.

- **Don't over complicate**

  We all want people to be impressed with our knowledge of things, whether it's our products and services, British current affairs, the history of the Baltic States, key characters in Game of Thrones, or who won the FA Cup in 1899 (It was Sheffield United against Derby at Crystal Palace in front of 69,000 people. Just saying).

  Have you ever been at a trade show or exhibition and suffered what we call "Tech Attack"? You step onto a stand and ask an innocent question about their wares. Unfortunately, you didn't manage to pick the sales guy who would has given you a clear response, hoping that you could be a prospect. No, you get the technical bod whose mission in life is to imply just how clever he is. He doesn't ask you any questions by way of qualification. You are assailed by a stream of technical consciousness littered with acronyms and theories that you will never understand because this is not your world. It is his and he is happy in it. This is a fine and admirable thing. It is also why he is not a salesman.

- **Get rid of the clutter**

We all feel better when we've finally cleared up our desk/office/bedroom etc. The same goes for our mind and the way we think. It is all about focusing on our objective and not being distracted by the mess around it. Focus, solve it and take action.

- **Create an achievable To-Do List**

Writing a To-Do list is a great way of focusing our energy on the day ahead. But make sure it's an achievable list, or you will only succeed in demotivating yourself by not completing it. Less is more.

Write a list of everything you consider outstanding or necessary. Then read it again and be brutal. Take out the things that can wait and prioritise the points where momentum can most easily be produced. Then, at the beginning of the list, ahead of your priority tasks, write down two very small, simple points that will start the process. It could be "*Make tea and coffee for the team*" and "*Send note of congratulations to a colleague*". Strike a line through them on the page and you are off, productive and moving forward.

- **Stuff is a nuisance**

Having stuff, especially in today's materialistic society, is almost a necessity. But how much of this stuff do we need? Think about what makes you really happy. We mean deep-down happy. If you're honest with yourself, life is much more important than stuff. The simple things do count for so much more. Just a thought, and who knows where it will lead you?

Stress Management

SUPER POWER	SUPERHERO	SALES POWER	APPLICATION
Super Senses	Beast	**Understanding**	Understand and be kind to yourself. Keep everything in perspective. Sales are a good things but life is better

- **Do it for you**

  To repeat what we said at the beginning of this guide; with power comes great responsibility. As a budding superhero in your field, you have a responsibility to do the right thing not only for your customers, colleagues and friends but also – *and this is crucial* - for yourself. Quite simply, if you're not in good mental shape, then your powers will be diminished, your senses will be dulled, and opportunities will be missed.

  No-one ever said that sales was an easy option as a career. And those that did were lying.

  The hours are long; you are always thinking three or four steps ahead; you are constantly reading the people that you meet; the clock is always ticking against deadlines; your manager wants results; the CRM needs daily attention; you have a daily task to guide your support team towards closing the sale; you are managing your client, your colleagues, your superiors and those more junior than yourself; you are travelling motorways and airlines at odd hours to reach your meetings; you are writing presentations to address your customer's pain points; you have detailed preparation for sales and forecast meetings on a weekly basis; you are networking with peers and prospects two or three nights a week; you are solving issues and ensuring that they are properly addressed by your team; you are writing sales collateral that is eye-catching and innovative; you are second guessing your competitors; you are keeping on top of your social media output and staying up to date with others'; you are working with your project and technical teams to ensure smooth operations with your customer; you are working with your marketing team on sales campaigns and lead generation; you are writing bids and proposals that must be eloquent and constructive.....you get the picture.

And meanwhile, your performance is being assessed against target on a monthly basis so that if you have a slow month or two, you are made to feel (or impose upon yourself) an inevitable sense of failure.

And yet you are expected to smile through the day and be Mr Sales Superhero.

Let's face it, given what you have to cope with each day, a certain amount of stress is inevitable.

- **You're not saving lives here**

  The first thing to remember is that what you are doing for a living is not life-threatening. No-one is going to die. Keep it all in perspective. Stress may well engulf you at times; your boss, your colleagues, your target, your presentation, but in the grand scheme of things none of it is important.

  What *is* important is the love and security of your family. Nothing else matters. Take a deep breath and remember that.

- **Keep it in perspective**

  How do you want to be remembered when you leave this earth? Do you want to be remembered as the person who spent too much time in the office? The person who worked themself to death? No, you do not.

  You want to be remembered as a good, honest human being who worked hard, worked smart, had the respect of his peers, the respect of his customers, and who knew when to take his foot off the accelerator and get back to a basic, simple life outside the work environment. You are working to improve the lives of those you love, not living to work.

- **Stress will be there**

  The very nature of your chosen career means that a certain amount of stress will arise from time to time. We are simply not designed as human beings to withstand such a multiplicity of varied and consistent pressures, and at some point you may feel that you cannot cope, your adrenalin will surge, and you will experience an instinctive *"fight or flight"* feeling.

This is not a sign of weakness. It is perfectly natural and different people handle it in different ways. Some drink, some smoke, some run away, some go into denial, some fight, some hide, and some develop an obsession to mask their fear.

Stress is defined as a state of not feeling in control of your situation, your environment, and how you are perceived by others.

- **Remember who you are**
  Stress can manifest itself by an overwhelming sense of low self-esteem. This is your mind throwing a protective blanket over you so that you stay under the radar and out of any perceived danger.

  Try to understand what an amazing, unique person you are. No-one knows what you know; no-one loves you like your family does; and no-one has the right to disrespect or offend you.

  Life is simply too short. This life, depending on your beliefs, may or may not be a rehearsal so grab the bloody thing in two hands and understand what *is* important.

- **Be mindful**

  Mindfulness is a relatively new concept to the western world but has demonstrated remarkable results in the management of stress.

  Mindfulness is about living in the moment and properly observing the world around you. It is about being compassionate with yourself and letting the negative thoughts drift by you, as you observe them with curiosity, knowing that nothing is to be taken personally. It is about observing people with aggressive words and actions, and understanding their insecurities and reasons for acting in such a way.

  This is not a deep meditation technique, but we recommend that you look it up and read more on the subject. It will help you to remain calm and composed in both your work and personal life.

- **Sure signs of stress**

  While stress is medically diagnosed as a chemical imbalance in the brain; there are symptoms that you should be aware of, such as;

  - Difficulty in sleeping
  - Loss of appetite
  - Poor concentration
  - Lethargy
  - Unusual errors
  - Emotional outbursts
  - Alcohol or drug use
  - Over-sensitivity

  Again, any one or combination of these symptoms is not a sign of weakness. It simply means that you have overdone it and need a little assistance or rest from what you're doing. See your GP as soon as you can and take his advice. You will be over it in no time.

- **Stress reduction**

  There will be times when you need just to get away and breathe. Here are some simple stress reduction techniques that may work for you;

Smile	Simple but effective
Laugh	Releases helpful chemicals in your brain
Fresh Air	Leave your office and walk. Sit in the park. Look at the sky
Drink water	Rehydrate regularly; your brain can't function without it
Power nap	10 min silence with your eyes closed
Herbal tea	Mint, ginger or orange infusions will revive you

The key thing is to be kind to yourself and relax. Try to maintain a sense of quiet confidence and perspective. If it does get too much for you on any particular day, walk away, turn off your phone and gently remind yourself that you can be a superhero tomorrow.

Now get out there and use your Sales Powers!

Well, you've come this far, and we hope that valuable lessons have been learned or refreshed. When you think about it, the successful sales person has to be almost superhuman to withstand the pressures and expectations (both internal and external) and constant drive for results, all the while maintaining powers of composure, creativity and instinctive empathy that would defeat lesser mortals.

But you are not a mere mortal. You, my friend, are a true Sales Superhero!

So we wish you good luck, bon voyage, and may your superpower guide you ever onward to superherodom (love that word!)